Walter Bagehot, Alfred Marshall

The Postulates of English Political Economy

Students Edition

Walter Bagehot, Alfred Marshall

The Postulates of English Political Economy
Students Edition

ISBN/EAN: 9783744644884

Printed in Europe, USA, Canada, Australia, Japan

Cover: Foto ©Suzi / pixelio.de

More available books at **www.hansebooks.com**

THE POSTULATES

OF

ENGLISH POLITICAL ECONOMY

BY THE LATE

WALTER BAGEHOT

M.A. AND FELLOW OF UNIVERSITY COLLEGE, LONDON

STUDENT'S EDITION

WITH A PREFACE

BY

ALFRED MARSHALL

PROFESSOR OF POLITICAL ECONOMY, CAMBRIDGE

LONDON

LONGMANS, GREEN, AND CO.

1885

PREFACE.

MR. BAGEHOT left behind him some materials for a book which promised to make a landmark in the history of economics, by separating the use of the older, or Ricardian, economic reasonings from their abuse, and freeing them from the discredit into which they had fallen, through being often mis-applied. Unfortunately, he did not complete more than the examination of two of their postulates— the transferability of labour and capital. But these he treated with so much sagacity and suggestiveness as to give us great help in dealing with the others, and I have long been anxious that what he wrote about them should be published in a cheap form, so as to have a wide circulation among students.[1]

[1] They were originally published in the *Fortnightly Review* in 1876, and are republished with some other materials for the great book, as *Economic Studies,* by the late Walter Bagehot, M.A.

He was excellently qualified for the task he undertook. He had a well-trained scientific mind, and a large experience of city life. He was an independent thinker, and perfectly free in his criticisms; but he reverenced the great men who had gone before him, and knew nothing of the temptation to try to raise himself by disparaging them. Though he has shown more clearly than perhaps anyone else the danger of a careless application of theory, he saw with great distinctness the need of its aid in dealing with complex economic problems. 'If you attempt to solve such problems,' he says, 'without some apparatus of method, you are as sure to fail as if you try to take a modern military fortress—a Metz or a Belfort—by common assault.'

Perhaps there never was anyone better fitted to show the real bearing of Ricardian modes of reasoning on the practical problems of life, or to bring out the fundamental unity which, in spite of minor differences, connects all the true work of the present with that of the earlier generation of economists.

and Fellow of University College, London, edited by Richard H Hutton. Longmans, 1880.

And in reading these essays we must remember that they deal almost exclusively with one side of what he had to say. Here he has explained the danger of assuming that the changes which are made quickly among modern English business men have been made quickly in other places and other times. But what he has written proves that had he lived he would have thrown much light on the question how the rapid changes of modern city life may help us to understand, by analogy and indirect inference, the slow changes of a backward people.

ALFRED MARSHALL.

CAMBRIDGE: *July* 10, 1885.

CONTENTS.

THE POSTULATES

OF

ENGLISH POLITICAL ECONOMY.

ADAM SMITH completed the 'Wealth of Nations' in 1776, and our English Political Economy is therefore just a hundred years old. In that time it has had a wonderful effect. The life of almost everyone in England—perhaps of everyone—is different and better in consequence of it. The whole commercial policy of the country is not so much founded on it as instinct with it. Ideas which are paradoxes everywhere else in the world are accepted axioms here as results of it. No other form of political philosophy has ever had one thousandth part of the influence on us ; its teachings have settled down into the common sense of the nation, and have become irreversible.

We are too familiar with the good we have thus acquired to appreciate it properly. To do so we

B

should see what our ancestors were taught. The
best book on Political Economy published in England
before that of Adam Smith is Sir James Steuart's
' Inquiry,' a book full of acuteness, and written by a
man of travel and cultivation. And its teaching is
of this sort : ' In all trade two things are to be considered in the commodity sold. The first is the
matter ; the second is the labour employed to render
this matter useful. The matter exported from a
country is what the country loses ; the price of the
labour exported is what it gains. If the value of the
matter imported be greater than the value of what
is exported the country gains. If a greater value of
labour be imported than exported the country loses.
Why ? Because in the first case strangers must
have paid *in matter* the surplus of labour exported ;
and in the second place because the strangers must
have paid to strangers *in matter* the surplus of labour
imported. It is, therefore, a general maxim to dis-
courage the importation of work, and to encourage
the exportation of it.'

It was in a world where *this* was believed that
our present Political Economy began.

Abroad the influence of our English system has
of course not been nearly so great as in England itself. But even there it has had an enormous effect.

All the highest financial and commercial legislation
of the Continent has been founded upon it. As
curious a testimony perhaps as any to its power is to
be found in the memoir of Mollien—the financial
adviser of the first Napoleon, *le bon Mollien*, whom
nothing would induce him to discard because his
administration brought *francs*, whereas that of his
more showy competitors might after all end in *ideas*.
'It was then,' says Mollien, in giving an account of
his youth, 'that I read an English book of which
the disciples whom M. Turgot had left spake with
the greatest praise—the work of Adam Smith. I
had especially remarked how warmly the venerable
and judicious Malesherbes used to speak of it—this
book so deprecated by all the men of the old routine
who spoke of themselves so improperly as of the
school of Colbert. They seemed to have persuaded
themselves that the most important thing for our
nation was that not one *sou* should ever leave France :
that so long as this was so, the kind and the amount
of taxation, the rate of wages, the greater or less
perfection of industrial arts, were things of complete
indifference, provided always that one Frenchman
gained what another Frenchman lost.'

And he describes how the 'Wealth of Nations'
led him to abandon those absurdities and to substi-

tute the views with which we are now so familiar,
but on which the ' good Mollien ' dwells as on new
paradoxes. In cases like this, one instance is worth
a hundred arguments. We see in a moment the
sort of effect that our English Political Economy has
had when we find it guiding the finance of Napoleon,
who hated ideologues, and who did not love the
English.

But notwithstanding these triumphs, the position of our Political Economy is not altogether satis-
factory. It lies rather dead in the public mind.
Not only does it not excite the same interest as
formerly, but there is not exactly the same confidence
in it. Younger men either do not study it, or do
not feel that it comes home to them, and that it
matches with their most living ideas. New sciences
have come up in the last few years with new
modes of investigation, and they want to know
what is the relation of economic science, as their
fathers held it, to these new thoughts and these new
instruments. They ask, often hardly knowing it,
will this ' science ' as it claims to be, harmonise with
what we now know to be sciences, or bear to be tried
as we now try sciences ? And they are not sure of
the answer.

Abroad, as is natural, the revolt is more avowed.

Indeed, though the Political Economy of Adam Smith penetrated deep into the Continent, what has been added in England since has never penetrated equally; though if our 'science' is true, the newer work required a greater intellectual effort, and is far more complete as a scientific achievement than anything which Adam Smith did himself. Political Economy, as it was taught by Ricardo, has had in this respect much the same fate as another branch of English thought of the same age, with which it has many analogies—jurisprudence as it was taught by Austin and Bentham; it has remained insular. I do not mean that it was not often read and understood; of course it was so, though it was often misread and misunderstood. But it never at all reigned abroad as it reigns here; never was really fully accepted in other countries as it was here where it arose. And no theory, economic or political, can now be both insular and secure; foreign thoughts come soon and trouble us; there will always be doubt here as to what is only believed here.

There are, no doubt, obvious reasons why English Political Economy should be thus unpopular out of England. It is known everywhere as the theory 'of Free-trade,' and out of England Free-trade is almost everywhere unpopular. Experience shows that no belief is so difficult to create, and no one so easy to disturb. The Protectionist creed rises like a weed in every soil. 'Why,' M. Thiers was asked, 'do you give these bounties to the French sugar-refiners?' 'I wish,' replied he, 'the tall chimneys to smoke.'. Every nation wishes prosperity for some conspicuous industry. At what cost to the consumer, by what hardship to less conspicuous industries, that prosperity is obtained, it does not care. Indeed, it hardly knows, it will never read, it will never apprehend the refined reasons which prove those evils and show how great they are; the visible picture of the smoking chimneys absorbs the whole mind. And, in many cases, the eagerness of England in the Free-trade cause only does that cause harm. Foreigners say, 'Your English traders are strong and rich; of course you wish to under-sell our traders, who are weak and poor. You have invented this Political Economy to enrich yourselves and ruin us; we will see that you shall not do so.'

And that English Political Economy is more opposed to the action of Government in all ways than most such theories, brings it no accession of popularity. All Governments like to interfere; it elevates their position to make out that they can cure the evils of mankind. And all zealots wish they should interfere, for such zealots think they can and may convert the rulers and manipulate the State control : it is a distinct object to convert a definite man, and if he will not be convinced there is always a hope of his successor. But most zealots dislike to appeal to the mass of mankind; they know instinctively that it will be too opaque and impenetrable for them.

Still I do not believe that these are the only reasons why our English Political Economy is not estimated at its value abroad. I believe that this arises from its special characteristic, from that which constitutes its peculiar value, and, paradoxical as it may seem, I also believe that this same characteristic is likewise the reason why it is often not thoroughly understood in England itself. The science of Political Economy as we have it in England may be defined as the science of business, such as business is in large productive and trading communities. It is an analysis of that world so familiar to many Englishmen—the 'great commerce' by which England has become rich. It assumes the principal facts which make that commerce possible, and as is the way of an abstract science it isolates and simplifies them : it detaches them from the confusion with which they are mixed in fact. And it deals too with the men who carry on that commerce, and who make it possible. It assumes a sort of human nature such as we see everywhere around us, and again it simplifies that human nature; it looks at one part of it only. Dealing with matters of 'business,' it assumes that man is actuated only by motives of business. It assumes that every man who makes anything, makes it for money, that he always makes that which brings him in most at least cost, and that he will make it in the way that will produce most and spend least; it assumes that every man who buys, buys with his whole heart, and that he who sells, sells with his whole heart, each wanting to gain all possible advantage. Of course we know that this is not so, that men are not like this; but we assume it for simplicity's sake, as an hypothesis. And this deceives many excellent people, for from deficient education they have very indistinct ideas what an abstract science is.

More competent persons, indeed, have understood that English Political Economists are not speaking of real men, but of imaginary ones: not of men as we see them, but of men as it is convenient to us to suppose they are. But even they often do not understand that the world which our Political Economists treat of, is a very limited and peculiar world also.

They often imagine that what they read is applicable to all states of society, and to all equally, whereas it is only true of—and only proved as to—states of society in which commerce has largely developed, and where it has taken the form of development, or something near the form, which it has taken in England.

This explains why abroad the science has not been well understood. Commerce, as we have it in England, is not so full-grown anywhere else as it is here—at any rate, is not so outside the lands populated by the Anglo-Saxon race. Here it is not only a thing definite and observable, but about the most definite thing we have, the thing which it is most difficult to help seeing. But on the Continent, though there is much that is like it, and though that much is daily growing more, there is nowhere the same pervading entity—the same patent, pressing, and unmistakable object.

And this brings out too the inherent difficulty of the subject—a difficulty which no other science, I think, presents in equal magnitude. Years ago I heard Mr. Cobden say at a League Meeting that 'Political Economy was the highest study of the human mind, for that the physical sciences required by no means so hard an effort.' An orator cannot be expected to be exactly precise, and of course

Political Economy is in no sense the highest study
of the mind—there are others which are much
higher, for they are concerned with things much
nobler than wealth or money; nor is it true that
the effort of mind which Political Economy requires
is nearly as great as that required for the abstruser
theories of physical science, for the theory of gravitation, or the theory of natural selection; but,
nevertheless, what Mr. Cobden meant had—as was
usual with his first-hand mind—a great fund of
truth.   He meant that Political Economy—effectual
Political Economy, Political Economy which in
complex problems succeeds—is a very difficult thing;
something altogether more abstruse and difficult, as
well as more conclusive, than that which many of
those who rush in upon it have a notion of.   It is
an abstract science which labours under a special
hardship.   Those who are conversant with its abstractions are usually without a true contact with its
facts; those who are in contact with its facts have
usually little sympathy with and little cognisance of
its abstractions.   Literary men who write about it
are constantly using what a great teacher calls 'un-
real words'—that is, they are using expressions with
which they have no complete vivid picture to corre-
spond.   They are like physiologists who have never

dissected; like astronomers who have never seen the stars; and, in consequence, just when they seem to be reasoning at their best, their knowledge of the facts falls short. Their primitive picture fails them, and their deduction altogether misses the mark—sometimes, indeed, goes astray so far, that those who live and move among the facts boldly say that they cannot comprehend 'how any one can talk such nonsense.' Yet, on the other hand, these people who live and move among the facts often, or mostly, cannot of themselves put together any precise reasonings about them. Men of business have a solid judgment—a wonderful guessing power of what is going to happen —each in his own trade; but they have never practised themselves in reasoning out their judgments and in supporting their guesses by argument: probably if they did so some of the finer and correcter parts of their anticipations would vanish. They are like the sensible lady to whom Coleridge said, 'Madam, I accept your conclusion, but you must let me find the logic for it.' Men of business can no more put into words much of what guides their life than they could tell another person how to speak their language. And so the 'theory of business' leads a life of obstruction, because theorists do not see the business, and the men of business will not reason out the theories.

Far from wondering that such a science is not completely perfect, we should rather wonder that it exists at all.

Something has been done to lessen the difficulty by statistics. These give tables of facts which help theoretical writers and keep them straight, but the cure is not complete. Writers without experience of trade are always fancying that these tables mean something more than, or something different from, that which they really mean. A table of prices, for example, seems an easy and simple thing to understand, and a whole literature of statistics assumes that simplicity : but in fact there are many difficulties. At the outset there is a difference between the men of theory and the men of practice. Theorists take a table of prices as facts settled by unalterable laws ; a stockbroker will tell you such prices can be 'made.' In actual business such is his constant expression. If you ask him what is the price of such a stock, he will say, if it be a stock at all out of the common, 'I do not know, sir : I will go on to the market and get them to *make* me a price.' And the following passage from the Report of the late Foreign Loans Committee shows what sort of process 'making' a price sometimes is :—'Immediately,' they say, 'after the publication of the prospectus '—the case is

that of the Honduras Loan —'and before any allotment was made, M. Lefevre authorised extensive pur-
chases and sales of loans on his behalf, brokers were
employed by him to deal in the manner best calculated
to maintain the price of the stock; the brokers so
employed instructed jobbers to purchase the stock
when the market required to be strengthened, and to
sell it if the market was sufficiently firm. In consequence of the market thus created dealings were carried on to a very large amount. Fifty or a hundred
men were in the market dealing with each other and
the brokers all round. One jobber had sold the loan
(2,500,000*l.*) once over.'

Much money was thus abstracted from credulous
rural investors ; and I regret to say that book statists
are often equally, though less hurtfully, deceived.
They make tables in which artificial prices run side
by side with natural ones; in which the price of an
article like Honduras scrip, which can be indefinitely
manipulated, is treated just like the price of Consols,
which can scarcely be manipulated at all. In most
cases it never occurs to the maker of the table that
there could be such a thing as an artificial—a *malâ
fide*—price at all. He imagines all prices to be
equally straightforward. Perhaps, however, this may
be said to be an unfair sample of price difficulties,

because it is drawn from the Stock Exchange, the
most complex market for prices ;—and no doubt the
Stock Exchange has its peculiar difficulties, of which
I certainly shall not speak lightly ; but on the other
hand, in one cardinal respect, it is the simplest of
markets.   There is no question in it of the physical
quality of commodities : one Turkish bond of 1858
is as good or bad as another ; one ordinary share in
a railway exactly the same as any other ordinary
share ; but in other markets each sample differs in
quality, and it is a learning in each market to judge
of qualities, so many are they, and so fine their gra-
dations.   Yet mere tables do not tell this, and cannot
tell it.   Accordingly in a hundred cases you may
see ' prices ' compared as if they were prices of the
same thing, when, in fact, they are prices of different
things.   The *Gazette* average of corn is thus compared incessantly, yet it is hardly the price of the
same exact quality of corn in any two years.   It is
an average of all the prices in all the sales in all the
markets.   But this year the kind of corn mostly sold
may be very superior, and last year very inferior—
yet the tables compare the two without noticing the
difficulty.   And when the range of prices runs over
many years, the figures are even more treacherous,
for the names remain, while the quality, the thing

signified, is changed. And of this persons not engaged in business have no warning. Statistical tables, even those which are most elaborate and careful, are not substitutes for an actual cognisance of the facts : they do not, as a rule, convey a just idea of the movements of a trade to persons not *in* the trade.

It will be asked, why do you frame such a science if from its nature it is so difficult to frame it ? The answer is that it is necessary to frame it, or we must go without important knowledge. The facts of commerce, especially of 'the great commerce,' are very complex. Some of the most important are not on the surface ; some of those most likely to confuse *are* on the surface. If you attempt to solve such problems without some apparatus of method, you are as sure to fail as if you try to take a modern military fortress—a Metz or a Belfort—by common assault ; you must have guns to attack the one, and method to attack the other.

The way to be sure of this is to take a few new problems, such as are for ever presented by investigation and life, and to see what by mere common sense we can make of them. For example, it is said that the general productiveness of the earth is less or more in certain regular cycles, corresponding with perceived changes in the state of the sun,—what would be the effect of this cyclical variation in the efficiency of industry upon commerce? Some hold, and as I think hold justly, that, extraordinary as it may seem, these regular changes in the sun have much to do with the regular recurrence of difficult times in the money market. What common sense would be able to answer these questions? Yet we may be sure that if there be a periodical series of changes in the yielding power of this planet, that series will have many consequences on the industry of men, whether those which have been suggested or others.

Or to take an easier case, who can tell without instruction what is likely to be the effect of the new loans of England to foreign nations? We press upon half-finished and half-civilised communities incalculable sums; we are to them what the London money-dealers are to students at Oxford and Cambridge. We enable these communities to read in every newspaper that they can have ready money, almost of any amount, on 'personal security.' No incipient and no arrested civilisations ever had this facility before. What will be the effect on such civilisations now, no untutored mind can say.

Or again: since the Franco-German War an

immense sum of new money has come to England; England has become the settling-place of international bargains much more than it was before; but whose mind could divine the effect of such a change as this, except it had a professed science to help it?

There are indeed two suggested modes of investigation, besides our English Political Economy, and competing with it. One is the Enumerative, or, if I may coin such a word, the 'All-case method.' One school of theorists say, or assume oftener than they say, that you should have a 'complete experience;' that you should accumulate all the facts of these subjects before you begin to reason. A very able German writer has said, in the 'Fortnightly Review,'[1] of a great economical topic, banking,—' I venture to suggest that there is but one way of arriving at such knowledge and truth'—that is absolute truth and full knowledge — ' namely, a thorough investigation of the facts of the case. By the facts, I mean not merely such facts as present themselves to so-called practical men in the common routine of business, but the facts which a complete historical and statistical inquiry would develop. When such a work shall have been accomplished, German economists may boast of having restored the prin-

---

[1] *Fortnightly Review* for September 1873.

ciples of banking, that is to say, of German banking, but not even then of banking in general. To set forth principles of banking in general, it will be necessary to master in the same way the facts of English, Scotch, French, and American banking, in short, of every country where banking exists.' 'The only,' he afterwards continues, 'but let us add also, the safe ground of hope for political economy, is, following Bacon's exhortation, to recommence afresh the whole work of economic inquiry. In what condition would chemistry, physics, geology, zoology be, and the other branches of natural science which have yielded such prodigious results, if their students had been linked to their chains of deduction from the assumptions and speculations of the last century?'

But the reply is that the method which Mr. Cohn suggests was tried in physical science and failed. And it is very remarkable that he should not have remembered it as he speaks of Lord Bacon, for the method which he suggests is exactly that which Lord Bacon himself followed, and owing to the mistaken nature of which he discovered nothing. The investigation into the nature of heat in the *Novum Organum* is exactly such a collection of facts as Mr. Cohn suggests,—but nothing comes of it. As Mr. Jevons well says, 'Lord Bacon's notion of scientific method was that of a kind of scientific book-keeping. Facts were to be indiscriminately gathered from every source, and posted in a kind of ledger from which would emerge in time a clear balance of truth. It is difficult to imagine a less likely way of arriving at discoveries.' And yet it is precisely that from which, mentioning Bacon's name, but not forewarned by his experience, Mr. Cohn hopes to make them.

The real plan that has answered in physical science is much simpler. The discovery of a law of nature is very like the discovery of a murder. In the one case you arrest a suspected person, and in the other you isolate a suspected cause. When Newton, by the fall of the apple, or something else, was led to think that the attraction of gravitation would account for the planetary motions, he took that cause by itself, traced out its effects by abstract mathematics, and so to say, found it ' guilty,'—he discovered that it would produce the phenomenon under investigation. In the same way Geology has been revolutionised in our own time by Sir Charles Lyell. He for the first time considered the effects of one particular set of causes by themselves. He showed how large a body of facts could be explained on the hypothesis ' that the forces now operating upon and beneath the earth's surface are the same both in kind and degree

as those which, at remote epochs, have worked out
geological changes.' He did not wait to begin his
inquiry till his data about all kinds of strata, or even
about any particular kind, were complete ; he took
palpable causes as he knew them, and showed how
many facts they would explain; he spent a long and
most important life in fitting new facts into an abstract and youthful speculation.   Just so in an instance which has made a literature and gone the round
of the world. Mr. Darwin, who is a disciple of Lyell,
has shown how one *vera causa*, 'natural selection,'
would account for an immense number of the facts of
nature ; for how many, no doubt, is controverted, but,
as is admitted, for a very large number.   And this he
showed by very difficult pieces of reasoning which very
few persons would have thought of, and which most
people found at first not at all easy to comprehend.
The process by which physical science has become
what it is, has not been that of discarding abstract
speculations, but of working out abstract speculations.   The most important known laws of nature—
the laws of motion—the basis of the figures in the
' Nautical Almanack ' by which every ship sails,—are
difficult and abstract enough, as most of us found to
our cost in our youth.

    There is no doubt a strong tendency to revolt

against abstract reasoning. Human nature has a strong ' factish ' element in it. The reasonings of the *Principia* are now accepted. But in the beginning they were ' mere crotchets of Mr. Newton's; ' Flamstead, the greatest astronomical discoverer of his day —the man of facts, *par excellence*—so called them ; they have irresistibly conquered ; but at first even those most conversant with the matter did not believe them. I do not claim for the conclusions of English Political Economy the same certainty as for the 'laws of motion.' But I say that the method by which they have been obtained is the same, and that the difference in the success of the two investigations largely comes from this—that the laws of wealth are the laws of a most complex phenomenon which you can but passively observe, and on which you cannot try experiments for science' sake, and that the laws of motion relate to a matter on which you can experiment, and which is comparatively simple in itself.

And to carry the war into the enemy's country, I say also that the method proposed by Mr. Cohn, the ' all case ' method is impossible. When I read the words ' all the facts of English banking,' I cannot but ask of what facts is Mr. Cohn thinking. Banking in England goes on growing, multiplying, and changing,

as the English people itself goes on growing, multiplying, and changing. The facts of it are one thing to-day
and another to-morrow; nor at one moment does any
one know them completely. Those who best know
many of them will not tell them or hint at them; gradually and in the course of years they separately come to
light, and by the time they do so, for the most part,
another crop of unknown ones has accumulated. If
we wait to reason till the 'facts' are complete, we
shall wait till the human race has expired. I think
that Mr. Cohn, and those who think with him, are
too 'bookish' in this matter. They mean by having
all the 'facts' before them, having all the printed
facts, all the statistical tables. But what has been said
of Nature is true of Commerce. 'Nature,' says Sir
Charles Lyell, 'has made it no part of her concern to
provide a record of her operations for the use of men;'
nor does trade either—only the smallest of fractions
of actual transactions is set down so that investigation
can use it. Literature has been called the 'fragment
of fragments,' and in the same way statistics are the
'scrap of scraps.' In real life scarcely any one knows
more than a small part of what his neighbour is doing,
and he scarcely makes public any of that little, or of
what he does himself. A complete record of commercial facts, or even of one kind of such facts, is the

completest of dreams. You might as well hope for
an entire record of human conversation.

There is also a second antagonistic method to that
of English Political Economy, which, by contrast, I
will call the 'single case' method. It is said that
you should analyse each group of facts separately—
that you should take the panic of 1866 separately,
and explain it; or, at any rate, the whole history of
Lombard Street separately, and explain it. And this
is very good and very important; but it is no
substitute for a preliminary theory. You might as
well try to substitute a corollary for the proposition
on which it depends. The history of a panic is the
history of a confused conflict of many causes; and
unless you know what sort of effect each cause is
likely to produce, you cannot explain any part of
what happens. It is trying to explain the bursting
of a boiler without knowing the theory of steam. Any
history of similar phenomena like those of Lombard
Street could not be usefully told, unless there was a
considerable accumulation of applicable doctrine
before existing. You might as well try to write the
'life' of a ship, making as you went along the theory
of naval construction. Clumsy dissertations would
run all over the narrative and the result would be
a perfect puzzle.

I have been careful not to use in this discussion
of methods the phrase which is oftenest used, viz.,
the Historical method, because there is an excessive
ambiguity in it. Sometimes it seems what I have
called the Enumerative, or, 'all case' method; sometimes the 'single case' method; a most confusing
double meaning, for by the mixture of the two the
mind is prevented from seeing the defects of either.
And sometimes it has other meanings, with which,
as I shall show, I have no quarrel, but rather much
sympathy. Rightly conceived, the Historical method
is no rival to the abstract method rightly conceived.

This conclusion is confirmed by a curious circum-
stance. At the very moment that our Political
Economy is objected to in some quarters as too abstract, in others an attempt is made to substitute for
it one which is more abstract still. Mr. Stanley
Jevons, and M. Walras, of Lausanne, without com-
munication, and almost simultaneously, have worked
out a 'mathematical' theory of Political Economy;—
and any one who thinks what is ordinarily taught in
England objectionable, because it is too little concrete in its method, and looks too unlike life and
business, had better try the new doctrine, which he
will find to be much worse on these points than the
old.

But I shall be asked, Do you then say that English Political Economy is perfect?—surely it is contrary to reason that so much difficulty should be felt in accepting a real science properly treated? At the first beginning no doubt there are difficulties in gaining a hearing for all sciences, but English Political Economy has long passed out of its first beginning? Surely, if there were not some intrinsic defect, it would have been firmly and coherently established, just as others are?

In this reasoning there is evident plausibility, and I answer that, in my judgment, there are three defects in the mode in which Political Economy has been treated in England, which have prevented people from seeing what it really is, and from prizing it at its proper value.

First,—It has often been put forward, not as a theory of the principal causes affecting wealth in *certain* societies, but as a theory of the principal, sometimes even of all, the causes affecting wealth in *every* society. And this has occasioned many and strong doubts about it. Travellers fresh from the sight, and historians fresh from the study, of peculiar and various states of society, look with dislike and disbelief on a single set of abstract propositions which claim, as they think, to be applicable to all

such societies, and to explain a most important part
of most of them.   I cannot here pause to say how
far particular English Economists have justified this
accusation; I only say that, taking the whole body
of them, there is much ground for it, and that in
almost every one of them there is some ground.   No
doubt almost every one—every one of importance—
has admitted that there is a 'friction' in society
which counteracts the effect of the causes treated of.
But in general they leave their readers with the
idea that, after all, this friction is but subordinate;
that probably in the course of years it may be
neglected; and, at any rate, that the causes assigned
in the science of Political Economy, as they treat it,
are the main and principal ones.   Now I hold that
these causes are only the main ones in a single kind
of society—a society of grown-up competitive commerce, such as we have in England; that it is only
in such societies that the other and counteracting
forces can be set together under the minor head of
'friction;' but that in other societies these other
causes—in some cases one, and in some another—
are the most effective ones, and that the greatest
confusion arises if you try to fit on *un*-economic
societies the theories only true of, and only proved
as to, economic ones.   In my judgment, we need—

not that the authority of our Political Economy should be impugned, but that it should be *minimised*; that we should realise distinctly where it is established, and where not; that its sovereignty should be upheld, but its frontiers marked. And until this is done, I am sure that there will remain the same doubt and hesitation in many minds about the science that there is now.

Secondly,—I think in consequence of this defect of conception Economists have been far more abstract, and in consequence much more dry, than they need have been. If they had distinctly set before themselves that they were dealing only with the causes of wealth in a single set of societies, they might have effectively pointed their doctrines with facts from those societies. But, so long as the vision of universal theory vaguely floated before them, they shrank from particular illustrations. Real societies are plainly so many and so unlike, that an instance from one kind does not show that the same thing exists in other societies;—it rather raises in the mind a presumption that it does not exist there; and therefore speculators aiming at an all-embracing doctrine refrain from telling cases, because those cases are apt to work in unexpected ways, and to raise up the image not only of the societies in which the tenet illustrated is true, but also of the opposite group in which it is false.

Thirdly,—It is also in consequence, as I imagine, of this defective conception of their science, that English Economists have not been so fertile as they should have been in verifying it. They have been too content to remain in the ' abstract,' and to shrink from concrete notions, because they could not but feel that many of the most obvious phenomena of many nations did not look much like their abstractions. Whereas in the societies with which the science is really concerned, an almost infinite harvest of verification was close at hand, ready to be gathered in; and because it has not been used, much confidence in the science has been lost, and it is thought ' to be like the stars which give no good light because they are so high.'

Of course this reasoning implies that the boundaries of this sort of Political Economy are arbitrary, and might be fixed here or there. But this is already implied when it is said that Political Economy is an abstract science. All abstractions are arbitrary; they are more or less convenient fictions made by the mind for its own purposes. An abstract idea means a concrete fact or set of facts *minus* something thrown away. The fact or set of facts were made by nature;

but how much you will throw aside of them and how much you will keep for consideration you settle for yourself. There may be any number of political economies according as the subject is divided off in one way or in another, and in this way all may be useful if they do not interfere with one another, or attempt to rule further than they are proved.

The particular Political Economy which I have been calling the English Political Economy is that of which the first beginning was made by Adam Smith. But what he did was much like the rough view of the first traveller who discovers a country ; he saw some great outlines well, but he mistook others and left out much. It was Ricardo who made the first map ; who reduced the subjects into consecutive shape, and constructed what you can call a science. Few greater efforts of mind have been made, and not many have had greater fruits. From Ricardo the science passed to a whole set of minds —James Mill, Senior, Torrens, Macculloch, and others, who busied themselves with working out his ideas, with elaborating and with completing them. For five-and-twenty years the English world was full of such discussions. Then Mr. J. S. Mill—the Mr. Mill whom the present generation know so well, and who has had so much influence,--shaped with masterly literary skill the confused substance of those discussions into a compact whole. He did not add a great deal which was his own, and some of what is due to him does not seem to me of great value. But he pieced the subjects together, showed where what one of his predecessors had done had fitted on to that of another, and adjusted this science to other sciences according to the notions of that time. To many students his book is the Alpha and Omega of Political Economy; they know little of what was before, and imagine little which can come after in the way of improvement. But it is not given to any writer to occupy such a place. Mr. Mill would have been the last to claim it for himself. He well knew that, taking his own treatise as the standard, what he added to Political Economy was not a ninth of what was due to Ricardo, and that for much of what is new in his book he was rather the *Secrétaire de la Rédaction*, expressing and formulating the current views of a certain world, than producing by original thought from his own brain. And his remoteness from mercantile life, and I should say his enthusiastic character, eager after things far less sublunary than money, made him little likely to give finishing touches to a theory of ' the great commerce.' In fact he has not done so ;

much yet remains to be done in it as in all sciences. Mr. Mill, too, seems to me open to the charge of having widened the old Political Economy either too much or not enough. If it be, as I hold, a theory proved of, and applicable to, particular societies only, much of what is contained in Mr. Mill's book should not be there; if it is, on the contrary, a theory holding good for all societies, as far as they are concerned with wealth, much more ought to be there, and much which is there should be guarded and limited. English Political Economy is not a finished and completed theory, but the first lines of a great analysis which has worked out much, but which still leaves much unsettled and unexplained.

There is nothing capricious, we should observe, in this conception of Political Economy, nor, though it originated in England, is there anything specially English in it. It is the theory of commerce, as commerce tends more and more to be when capital increases and competition grows. England was the first—or one of the first—countries to display these characteristics in such vigour and so isolated as to suggest a separate analysis of them, but as the world goes on, similar characteristics are being evolved in one society after another. A similar money market, a similar competing trade based on

large capital, gradually tends to arise in all countries.
As 'men of the world' are the same everywhere,
so 'the great commerce' is the same everywhere.
Local peculiarities and ancient modifying circumstances fall away in both cases ; and it is of this one
and uniform commerce which grows daily, and which
will grow, according to every probability, more and
more, that English Political Economy aspires to be
the explanation.

And our Political Economy does not profess to
prove this growing world to be a good world—far
less to be the best. Abroad the necessity of con-
testing socialism has made some writers use the
conclusions brought out by our English science for
that object. But the aim of that science is far more
humble ; it says these and these forces produce these
and these effects, and there it stops. It does not
profess to give a moral judgment on either ; it
leaves it for a higher science, and one yet more
difficult, to pronounce what ought and what ought
not to be.

The first thing to be done for English Political
Economy, as I hold, is to put its aim right. So long
as writers on it do not clearly see, and as readers do
not at all see, the limits of what they are analysing,
the result will not satisfy either. The science will

continue to seem what to many minds it seems now,
proved perhaps, but proved *in nubibus*; true, no
doubt, somehow and somewhere, but that somewhere
a *terra incognita*, and that somehow an unknown
quantity.—As a help in this matter I propose to take
the principal assumptions of Political Economy one
by one, and to show, not exhaustively, for that would
require a long work, but roughly, where each is true
and where it is not. We shall then find that our
Political Economy is not a questionable thing of
unlimited extent, but a most certain and useful thing
of limited extent. By marking the frontier of our
property we shall learn its use, and we shall have a
positive and reliable basis for estimating its value.

I.

THE TRANSFERABILITY OF LABOUR.

THE first assumption which I shall take is that
which is perhaps oftener made in our economic
reasonings than any other, namely, that labour (mas-
culine labour, I mean) and capital circulate readily
within the limits of a nation from employment to
employment, leaving that in which the remuneration
is smaller and going to that in which it is greater.
No assumption can be better founded, as respects
such a country as England, in such an economic
state as our present one. A rise in the profits of
capital, in any trade, brings more capital to it with
us now-a-days—I do not say quickly, for that would
be too feeble a word, but almost instantaneously. If,
owing to a high price of corn, the corn trade on a
sudden becomes more profitable than usual, the bill-
cases of bill-brokers and bankers are in a few days
stuffed with corn-bills—that is to say, the free
capital of the country is by the lending capitalists,

the bankers and bill-brokers, transmitted where it is
most wanted. When the price of coal and iron rose
rapidly a few years since, so much capital was found
to open new mines and to erect new furnaces that
the profits of the coal and iron trades have not yet
recovered it. In this case the influence of capital
attracted by high profits was not only adequate but
much more than adequate : instead of reducing these
profits only to an average level, it reduced them below
that level ; and this happens commonly, for the
speculative enterprise which brings in the new capital
is a strong, eager, and rushing force, and rarely stops
exactly where it should. Here and now a craving for
capital in a trade is almost as sure to be followed by
a plethora of it as winter to be followed by summer.
Labour does not flow so quickly from pursuit to
pursuit, for man is not so easily moved as money—
but still it moves very quickly. Patent statistical
facts show what we may call 'the tides' of our
people. Between the years shown by the last census,
the years 1861 and 1871, the population of

The Northern counties increased 23 per cent.
Yorkshire   „   19   „
North-Western counties   „   14   „
London   ,,   16   „

While that of

> The South-Western counties only increased 2 per cent.
> Eastern   „   „   7   „
> North Midland   „   „   9   „

—though the fertility of marriages is equal. The set of labour is steadily and rapidly from the counties where there is only agriculture and little to be made of new labour, towards those where there are many employments and where much is to be made of it.

No doubt there are, even at present in England, many limitations to this tendency, both of capital and of labour, which are of various degrees of importance, and which need to be considered for various purposes. There is a ' friction,' but still it is only a ' friction ; ' its resisting power is mostly defeated, and at a first view need not be regarded. But taking the world, present and past, as a whole, the exact contrary is true ; in most ages and countries this tendency has been not victorious but defeated ; in some cases, it can scarcely be said even to have existed, much less to have conquered. If you take at random a country in history, the immense chances are that you will find this tendency either to be altogether absent, or not at all to prevail as it does with us now. This primary assumption of our Political Economy is not true everywhere and always, but only in a few places and a few times.

The truth of it depends on the existence of conditions which, taken together, are rarely satisfied. Let us take labour first, as it is the older and simpler of the two. First, there must be 'employments' between which labour is to migrate; and this is not true at all of the primitive states of society. We are used to a society which abounds in felt wants that it can satisfy, and where there are settled combinations of men—trades, as we call them—each solely occupied in satisfying some one of them. But in primitive times nothing at all like this exists. The conscious wants of men are few, the means of supplying them still fewer, and the whole society homogeneous—one man living much as another. Civilisation is a shifting mixture of many colours, but barbarism was and is of a dull monotony, hardly varying even in shade.

A picture or two of savage tribes brings this home to the mind better than abstract words. Let us hear Mr. Catlin's description of a favourite North American tribe, with which he means us to be much pleased :—'The Mandans, like all other tribes, live lives of idleness and leisure, and of course devote a great deal of time to their amusements, of which

they have a great variety. Of these dancing is one
of the principal, and may be seen in a variety of
forms: such as the buffalo dance, the boasting dance,
the begging dance, the scalp dance, and a dozen other
dances, all of which have their peculiar characters
and meanings and objects.'

Then he describes the 'starts and jumps' of
these dances and goes on :—' Buffaloes, it is well
known, are a sort of roaming creatures congregating
occasionally in huge masses, and strolling away about
the country from east to west or from north to south,
or just where their whims or fancies may lead them;
and the Mandans are sometimes by this means most
unceremoniously left without anything to eat, and
being a small tribe and unwilling to risk their lives
by going far from home in the face of their more
powerful enemies, are oftentimes left almost in a
state of starvation. In any emergency of this kind
every man musters and brings out of his lodge his
mask (the skin of a buffalo's head with the horns on),
which he is obliged to keep in readiness for the
occasion ; and then commences the buffalo dance of
which I have spoken, which is held for the purpose
of making " buffalo come," as they term it—of in-
ducing the buffalo herds to change the direction of
their wanderings, and bend their course towards the

Mandan village and graze about on the beautiful hills and bluffs in its vicinity, where the Mandans can shoot them down and cook them as they want them for food. For the most part of the year the young warriors and hunters by riding out a mile or two from the village can kill meat in abundance; and sometimes large herds of these animals may be seen grazing in full view of the village. There are other seasons also when the young men have ranged about the country, as far as they are willing to risk their lives on account of their enemies, without finding meat. This sad intelligence is brought back to the chiefs and doctors, who sit in solemn council and consult on the most expedient measures to be taken until they are sure to decide the old and only expedient " which has never failed." This is the buffalo dance, which is incessantly continued till " buffalo come," and which the whole village by relays of dancers keeps up in succession. And when the buffaloes are seen, there is a brisk preparation for the chase—a great hunt takes place. The choicest pieces of the carcase are sacrificed to the Great Spirit, and then a surfeit or a carouse. These dances have sometimes been continued for two or three weeks until the joyful moment when buffaloes made their appearance. And so they "*never fail*," as the village thinks, to bring the buffaloes in.'

Such is the mode of gaining the main source of existence, without which the tribe would starve. And as to the rest we are told :—' The principal occupations of the women in this village consist in procuring wood and water, in cooking, dressing robes and other skins, in drying meat and wild fruits, and raising maize.'

In this attractive description there is hardly any mention of male labour at all ; the men hunt, fight, and amuse themselves, and the women do all the rest.

And in the lowest form of savage life, in the stone age, the social structure must have been still more uniform, for there were still less means to break or vary it. The number of things which can be made with a flint implement is much greater than one would have imagined, and savages made more things with it than anyone would make now. Time is nothing in the savage state, and protracted labour, even with the worst instrument, achieves much, especially when there are no other means of achieving anything. But there is no formal division of employments—no cotton trade, no iron trade, no woollen trade. There are beginnings of a division, of course, but as a rule, everyone does what he can at everything.

In much later times the same uniformity in the structure of society still continues. We all know from childhood how simple is the constitution of a pastoral society. As we see it in the Pentateuch it consists of one family, or a group of families, possessing flocks and herds, on which, and by which, they live. They have no competing employments; no alternative pursuits. What manufactures there are are domestic, are the work of women at all times, and of men, of certain men, at spare times. No circulation of labour is then conceivable, for there is no circle; there is no group of trades round which to go, for the whole of industry is one trade.

Many agricultural communities are exactly similar. The pastoral communities have left the life of movement, which is essential to a subsistence on the flocks and herds, and have fixed themselves on the soil. But they have hardly done more than change one sort of uniformity for another. They have become peasant proprietors—combining into a village, and holding more or less their land in common, but having no pursuit worth mentioning, except tillage. The whole of their industrial energy —domestic clothes-making and similar things excepted—is absorbed in that.

No doubt in happy communities a division of

labour very soon and very naturally arises, and at first sight we might expect that with it a circulation of labour would begin too. But an examination of primitive society does not confirm this idea; on the contrary, it shows that a main object of the social organisation which then exists, is to impede or prevent that circulation. And upon a little thought the reason is evident. There is no paradox in the notion; early nations were not giving up an advantage which they might have had; the good which we enjoy from the circulation of labour was unattainable by them; all they could do was to provide a substitute for it—a means of enjoying the advantages of the division of labour without it,— and this they did. We must carry back our minds to the circumstances of primitive society before we can comprehend the difficulty under which they laboured, and see how entirely it differs from any which we have to meet now.

A free circulation of labour from employment to employment involves an incessant competition between man and man, which causes constant quarrels,—some of which, as we see in the daily transactions of trades unions, easily run into violence; and also a constant series of new bargains, one differing from another, some of which are sure

to be broken, or said to be so, which makes disputes
of another kind. The peace of society was exposed
in early times to greater danger from this source
than now, because the passions of men were then
less under control than 'now. 'In the simple and
violent times,' as they have been well called, 'which
we read of in our Bibles,' people struck one another,
and people killed one another, for very little matters
as we should think them. And the most efficient
counteractive machinery which now preserves that
peace, then did not exist. We have now in the
midst of us a formed, elaborate, strong government,
which is incessantly laying down the best rules
which it can find to prevent trouble under changing
circumstances, and which constantly applies a sharp
pervading force running through society to prevent
and punish breaches of those rules.' We are so
familiar with the idea of a government inherently
possessing and daily exercising both executive and
legislative power, that we scarcely comprehend the
possibility of a nation existing without them. But
if we attend to the vivid picture given in the Book
of Judges of an early stage in Hebrew society, we
shall see that there was then absolutely no legislative
power, and only a faint and intermittent executive
power. The idea of law-making, the idea of making

new rules for new circumstances, would have been as incomprehensible to Gideon or Abimelech as the statutes at large to a child of three years old. They and their contemporaries thought that there was an unalterable law consecrated by religion and confirmed by custom which they had to obey, but they could not have conceived an alteration of it except as an act of wickedness—a worshipping of Baal. And the actual coercive power available for punishing breaches of it was always slight, and often broken. One 'judge,' or ruler, arises after another, sometimes in one tribe and place, and sometimes in another, and exercises some kind of jurisdiction, but his power is always limited; there is no organisation for transmitting it, and often there is no such person —no king in Israel whatever.

The names and the details of this book may or may not be historical, but its spirit is certainly true. The peace of society then reposed on a confused sentiment, in which respect for law, as such—at least law in our usual modern sense—was an inconsiderable element, and of which the main components were a coercive sense of ingrained usage, which kept men from thinking what they had not before thought, and from doing what they had not before done; a vague horror that something, they did not well know what, might happen if they did so; a close religion which filled the air with deities who were known by inherited tradition, and who hated uninherited ways; and a submission to local opinion inevitable when family and tribe were the main props of life,—when there really was 'no world without Verona's walls,'—when every exile was an outcast, expelled from what was then most natural, and scarcely finding an alternative existence.

No doubt this sentiment was in all communities partially reinforced by police. Even at the time of the 'Judges,' there were no doubt 'local authorities,' as we should now say, who forcibly maintained some sort of order even when the central power was weakest. But the main support of these authorities was the established opinion; they had no military to call in, no exterior force to aid them; if the fixed sentiment of the community was not strong enough to aid them, they collapsed and failed. But that fixed sentiment would have been at once weakened, if not destroyed, by a free circulation of labour, which is a spring of progress that is favourable to new ideas, that brings in new inventions, that prevents the son being where his father was, that interrupts the tradition of generations and breaks inherited feeling. Besides causing new sorts of quarrels by creating

new circumstances and new occasions, this change
of men from employment to employment decomposes
the moral authority which alone in this state of
society can prevent quarrels or settle them. Accordingly, the most successful early societies have for-
bidden this ready change as much as possible, and
have endeavoured, as far as they could, to obtain
the advantages of the division of labour without it.
Sir Henry Maine, to whom this subject so peculiarly
belongs, and who has taught us so much more on it
than any one else, shall describe the industrial ex-
pedients of primitive society as he has seen them
still surviving in India:—' There is,' he says, ' yet
another feature of the modern Indian cultivating
group which connects them with primitive western
communities of the same kind. I have several times
spoken of them as organised and self-acting. They,
in fact, include a nearly complete establishment of
occupations and trades for enabling them to continue
their collective life without assistance from any person or body external to them. Besides the headmen
or council exercising quasi-judicial, quasi-legislative
power, they contain a village police, now recognised
and paid in certain provinces by the British Government. They include several families of hereditary
traders; the blacksmith, the harness-maker, the

shoemaker. The Brahmin is also found for the per-
formance of ceremonies, and even the dancing-girl
for attendance at festivities. There is invariably a
village accountant, an important person among an
unlettered population, so important, indeed, and so
conspicuous, that, according to reports current in
India, the earliest English functionaries engaged in
settlements of land were occasionally led by their
assumption that there must be a single proprietor
somewhere to mistake the accountant for the owner
of the village, and to record him as such in the
official register. But the person practising any one
of these hereditary employments is really a servant
of the community as well as one of its component
members. He is sometimes paid by an allowance in
grain, more generally by the allotment to his family
of a piece of land in hereditary possession. Whatever else he may demand for the wares he produces
is limited by a fixed price very rarely departed
from.'

To no world could the free circulation of labour,
as we have it in England, and as we assume it in our
Political Economy, be more alien, and in none would
it have been more incomprehensible. In this case as
in many others, what seems in later times the most
natural organisation is really one most difficult to

create, and it does not arise till after many organisations which seem to our notions more complex have
preceded it and perished. The village association of
India, as Sir Henry Maine describes it, seems a much
more elaborate structure, a much more involved piece
of workmanship, than a common English village,
where everyone chooses his own calling, and where
there are no special rules for each person, and where
a single law rules all. But in fact our organisation
is the more artificial because it presupposes the pervading intervention of an effectual Government—the
last triumph of civilisation, and one to which early
times had nothing comparable. In expecting what
we call simple things from early ages, we are in fact
expecting them to draw a circle without compasses,
to produce the results of civilisation when they have
not attained civilisation.

One instance of this want of simplicity in early
institutions, which has, almost more than any other,
impaired the free transit of labour, is the complexity of the early forms of landholding. In a
future page I hope to say something of the general
effects of this complexity, and to compare it with the
assumptions as to ownership in land made by Ricardo
and others. I am here only concerned with it as
affecting the movement of men, but in this respect

its effect has been incalculable. As is now generally known, the earliest form of landowning was not individual holding, but tribal owning. In the old contracts of Englishmen with savages nothing was commoner than for the king or chief to sell tracts of land,—and the buyers could not comprehend that according to native notions he had no right to do so, that he could not make a title to it, and that according to those notions there was no one who could. Englishmen in all land dealings looked for some single owner, or at any rate some small number of owners, who had an exceptional right over particular pieces of land; they could not conceive the supposed ownership of a tribe, as in New Zealand, or of a village in India, over large tracts. Yet this joint-stock principle is that which has been by far the commonest in the world, and that which the world began with. And not without good reason. In the early ages of society, it would have been impossible to maintain the exclusive ownership of a few persons in what seems at first sight an equal gift to all—a thing to which everyone has the same claim. There was then no distinct government apart from and above the tribe any more than among New Zealanders now. There was no compulsory agency which could create or preserve exclusive ownership

of the land, even if it had been wished. And of
course it could not have been wished, for though
experience has now conclusively shown that such
exclusive ownership is desirable for and beneficial to
the nation as a whole, as well as to the individual
owner, no theorist would have been bold enough to
predict this beforehand. This monopoly is almost a
paradox after experience, and it would have seemed
monstrous folly before it. Indeed, the idea of a discussion of it, is attributing to people in the year
1000 B.C. the notions of people in the year 1800 A.D.
Common ownership was then irremediable and inevitable ; no alternative for it was possible, or would
then have been conceivable. But it is in its essence
opposed to the ready circulation of labour. Few
things fix a man so much as a share in a property
which is fixed by nature ; and common ownership,
wherever it prevails, gives the mass of men such a
share.

And there is another force of the same tendency
which does not act so widely, but which when it does
act is even stronger—in many cases is omnipotent.
This is the disposition of many societies to crystallise
themselves into *specialised* groups, which are definite
units, each with a character of its own, and are
more or less strictly hereditary. Sir Henry Maine has

described to us how in an Indian village the black-smith is hereditary, and the harness-maker, and the shoemaker,—and this is natural, for every trade has its secrets, which make a kind of craft or 'mystery' of it, and which must be learnt by transmission or not at all. ·The first and most efficient kind of apprenticeship is that by birth; the father teaches his son that by which he makes his living, almost without knowing it; the son picks up the skill which is in the air of the house, almost without feeling that he is doing so. Even now we see that there are city families, and university and legal families,—families where a special kind of taste and knowledge are passed on in each generation by tradition, and which in each have in that respect an advantage over others. In most ages most kinds of skilled labour have shown a disposition to intensify this advantage by combination—to form a bounded and exclusive society, guild, trades union, or whatever it may be called, which keeps or tries to keep in each case to itself the rich secret of the inherited art. And even when no pains are taken, each special occupation, after it gains a certain size, tends to form itself into a separate group. Each occupation has certain peculiar characteristics which help to success in it, and which, therefore, it fosters and develops; and in a subtle way these traits collect together and form a group-character analogous to a national character. The process of caste-making is often thought to be an old-world thing which came to an end when certain old castes were made and fixed before the dawn of history. But in fact the process has been actively at work in recent times, and has hardly yet died out. Thus in Cashmere, where the division of castes is already minute, Mr. Drew tells us that of the Batals —a class at the very bottom of the scale, 'whose trade it is to remove and skin carcasses, and to cure leather,'—he has heard 'that there are two classes; so apt are communities in India to divide and to sub-divide, to perpetuate differences, and to separate rather than amalgamate. The higher Batals follow the Mohammedan rules as to eating, and are allowed some fellowship with the other Mohammedans. The lower Batals eat carrion, and would not bear the name of Mohammedans in the mouths of others, though they might call themselves so.' Just so, Mr. Hunter says that 'the Brahmans of Lower Bengal bore to the Brahmans of Oudh the same relation that the landed gentry of Canada or Australia bears to the landed gentry of England. Each is an aristo-cracy, both claim the title of esquire, but each is composed of elements whose social history is widely different, and the home aristocracy never regards the successful settlers as equal in rank. The Brahmans of the midland land went further; they declared the Brahmans of Lower Bengal inferior not only in the social scale, but in religious capabilities. To this day many of the north country Brahmans do not eat with the Brahmans of the lower valley, and convicted felons from the north-west will suffer repeated floggings in jail, for contumacy, rather than let rice cooked by a Bengal Brahman pass their lips.' Caste-making is not a rare act, but a constantly occurring act, when circumstances aid it, and when the human mind is predisposed to it.

One great aid to this process is the mutual animosity of the different groups. 'What one nation hates,' said Napoleon, 'is another nation;' just so, what one caste hates is another caste : the marked characteristics of each form—by their difference—a certain natural basis for mutual dislike. There is an intense disposition in the human mind—as you may see in any set of schoolboys—to hate what is unusual and strange in other people, and each caste supplies those adjoining it with a conspicuous supply of what is unusual. And this hatred again makes each caste more and more unlike the other, for everyone wishes as much as possible to distinguish himself from the

neighbouring hated castes by excelling in the peculiarities of his own caste, and by avoiding theirs.

In the ancient parts of the world these contrasts
of group to group are more or less connected for the
most part with contrasts of race. Very often the
origin of the 'caste—the mental tendency which made
its first members take to its special occupation—was
some inborn peculiarity of race ; and at other times,
as successive waves of conquest passed over the
country, each race of conquerors connected themselves
most with, and at last were absorbed in, the pre-
existing kind of persons which they most resembled,
and frequently in so doing hardened into an absolute
caste what was before a half-joined and incipient
group.

Each conquest, too, tends to make a set of out-
casts—generally from the worst part of the previous
population—and these become ' hewers of wood and
drawers of water ' to the conquerors—that is, they are
an outlying and degraded race, which is not admitted
to compete or mix with the others, and which becomes
more degraded from feeling that it is thus inferior,
and from being confined to the harder, baser, and
less teaching occupations. And upon these unhappy
groups the contempt and hatred of the higher ones
tend to concentrate themselves, and, like most strong

sentiments in the early world, these feelings find for themselves a religious sanction. To many villages in India, Sir Henry Maine says, there are attached a class of 'outsiders' who never enter the village, or only enter reserved portions of it, who are looked on as 'essentially impure,' 'whose very touch is avoided as contaminating.' These poor people are more or less thought to be 'accursed;' to have some taint which shows that the gods hate them, and which justifies men in hating them too, and in refusing to mix with them.

The result of these causes is, that many ancient societies are complex pieces of patchwork—bits of contrasted human nature, put side by side. They have a variegated complexity, which modern civilised States mostly want. And there must clearly have been an advantage in this organisation of labour—to speak of it in modern phrase—though it seems to us now so strange, or it would not have sprung up independently in many places and many ages, and have endured in many for long tracts of years. This advantage, as we have seen, was the gain of the division of labour without the competition which with us accompanies it, but which the structure of society was not then hard enough to bear.

No doubt we must not push too far this notion of

the rigidity of caste. The system was too rigid to work without some safety-valves, and in every age and place where that system prevails, some have been provided. Thus in India we are told ' a Brahmana unable to subsist by his duties may live by the duty of a soldier ; if he cannot get a subsistence by either of these employments, he may apply to tillage and attendance on cattle, or gain a competence by traffic, avoiding certain commodities. A Ghatriya in distress may subsist by all these means, but he must not have recourse to the highest functions. A Vaisya unable to subsist by his own duties may descend to the servile acts of a Sudra ; and a Sudra, not finding employment by waiting on men of the higher classes, may subsist by handicrafts ; besides the particular occupations assigned to the mixed classes, they have the alternative of following that profession which regularly belongs to the class from which they derive their origin on the mother's side ; ' and so on, without end.

And probably it is through these supplementary provisions, as I may call them, that the system of caste ultimately breaks down and disappears. It certainly disappeared in ancient Egypt when the compact Roman Government was strong enough to do without it, and when a change of religion had removed the sanctions which fixed and consecrated it. The process is most slow, as our experience in India proves. The saying that ' La Providence a ses aises dans le temps ' has rarely elsewhere seemed so true. Still, the course is sure, and the caste system will in the end pass away, whenever an efficient substitute has been made for it, and the peace of industry secured without it.

But it would be a great mistake to believe that, whenever and wherever there is an efficient external government capable of enforcing the law, and of making the competitive migration of labour safe and possible, such migration of itself at once begins. There is, in most cases, a long and dreary economic interval to be passed first. In many countries, the beginning of such migration is for ages retarded by the want of another requisite—the want of external security. We have come in modern Europe to look on nations as if they were things indestructible—at least, on large nations. But this is a new idea, and even now it has to be taken with many qualifications. But in many periods of history it has not been true at all ; the world was in such confusion, that it was almost an even chance whether nations should continue, or whether they should be conquered and destroyed. In such times the whole energy of the community must be concentrated on its own defence ;

all that interferes with it must be sacrificed, if it is to
live. And the most efficient mode of defending it
is generally a feudal system ; that is, a local militia
based on the land, where each occupier of the soil
has certain services to render, of which he cannot
divest himself, and which he must stay on certain
fields to perform when wanted. In consequence the
races of men which were possessed of an organisation
easily adapting itself to the creation of such a militia,
have had a striking tendency to prevail in the strug-
gle of history. ' The feudal system,' says Sir George
Campbell, on many accounts one of our most competent judges, ' I believe to be no invention of the
Middle Ages, but the almost necessary result of the
hereditary character of the Indo-Germanic institutions, when the tribes take the position of dominant
conquerors. They form, in fact, an hereditary army,
with that gradation of fealty from the commander to
the private soldier which is essential in military operations. Accordingly, we find that among all the tribes
of Indo-Germanic blood which have conquered and
ruled Indian provinces, the tendency is to establish a
feudal system extremely similar to that which prevailed
in Europe. In Rajpootana the system is still in full
force. The Mahrattas and Sikhs had both established
a similar system. In my early days it existed in

great perfection in some parts of the Cis-Sutlej States.' And where the system is most developed, at the lowest point of the scale there is always an immovable class—serfs, *villeins regardants*, or what we choose to call them—who do not fight themselves, who perhaps are too abject in spirit, or perhaps are of too dubious fidelity to be let have arms, but who cultivate the ground for those who really fight. The soldier class, rooted to the land by martial tenure, has beneath it a non-soldier class even more rooted to the soil by the tenure of tilling it. I need not say how completely such a system of military defence, and such a system of cultivation, are opposed to the free transit of labour from employment to employment. Where these systems are perfectly developed, this transit is not so much impeded as prevented.

And there is a yet more pervading enemy of the free circulation of labour. This is slavery. We must remember that our modern notion that slavery is an exceptional institution, is itself an exceptional idea ; it is the product of recent times and recent philosophies. No ancient philosopher, no primitive community, would have comprehended what we meant by it. That human beings are divided into strong and weak, higher and lower, or what is thought to be such ; and that the weak and inferior ought to be made to serve the higher and better, whether they would wish to do so or not, are settled axioms of early thought. Whatever might be the origin and whatever might be the fate of other institutions, the ancient world did not doubt that slavery at all events existed ' by the law of nature,' and would last as long as men. And it interferes with the ready passage of labour from employment to employment in two ways. First, it prevents what we call for this purpose ' employments '—that is, markets where labour may be bought, mostly in order that the produce may be sold. Slavery, on the contrary, strengthens and extends domestic manufactures where the produce is never sold at all, where it is never intended to be so, but where each household by its own hands makes what it wants. In a slave-community so framed, not only is there little quick migration of free labour, but there are few fit places for it to migrate between ; there are no centres for the purchase of much of it ; society tends to be divided into self-sufficing groups, buying little from the exterior. And at a later stage of industrial progress slavery arrests the movement of free labour still more effectively by providing a substitute. It is, then, the slave labour which changes occupation, and not the free labour. Just as in the present day a capitalist who wants to execute any sort of work hires voluntary labour to do it, so in a former stage of progress he would buy slaves in order to do it. He might not, indeed, be able to buy enough slaves —enough suitable slaves, that is, for his purpose. The organisation of slavery has never been as effectual as our present classified system of free labour, and from intrinsic defects never can be. But it does develop earlier. Just when the system of free labour might develop if it were let alone, the imperfect substitute of slavery steps in and spoils it. When free labour still moves slowly and irregularly, and when frequent wars supply the slave-market with many prisoners, the slave-market is much the easiest resource of the capitalist. So it is when a good slave-trade keeps it well filled. The capitalist finds it better to buy than to hire, for there are in this condition of things comparatively many men to be bought and comparatively few to be hired. And the result takes unexpected directions. 'What the printing press is in modern times,' says a German writer, 'that slavery was in ancient times.' And though this may be a little exaggerated, it is certain that in ancient Rome books were produced much cheaper and in much greater number than they were for hundreds of years afterwards. When there was

a demand for a book, extra copying-slaves could be
'turned on' to multiply it in a way which in later
times, when slavery had ceased, was impossible, and
which is only surpassed by the way in which addi-
tional compositors are applied to works in demand
now. And political philosophers proposed to obtain
revenue from this source, and to save taxation.
'Suppose,' says Xenophon, 'that the Athenian State
should buy twelve thousand slaves, and should let
them out to work in the mines at an obolus a head,
and suppose that the whole amount annually thus
received should be employed in the purchase of new
slaves, who should again in the same way yield the
same income, and so on successively; the State
would then by these means in five or six years possess
six thousand slaves,' which would yield a large
income. The idea of a compound interest investment
in men, though abhorrent to us, seemed most natural
to Xenophon. And almost every page of the classics
proves how completely the civilisation then existing
was based on slavery in one or other of its forms—
that of skilled labour (the father of Demosthenes
owned thirty-three cutlers and twenty coachmakers)
or unskilled, that might either be worked by the
proprietor or let out, as he liked. Even if this
system had only economic consequences, it must

have prevented the beginning of freely moving labour, for it is much handier than such a system can be at its outset. And as we know, the system has moral effects working in the same way even more powerful, for it degrades labour by making it the slave-mark, and makes the free labourer—whether the *prolétaire* of ancient cities, or the 'mean white' of American plantations—one of the least respectable and the least workmanlike of mankind.

Happily this full-grown form of slavery is exceedingly frail. We have ourselves seen in America how completely it collapses at an extrinsic attack; how easy it is to destroy it, how impossible to revive it. And much of the weakness of ancient civilisation was also so caused. Any system which makes the mass of a society hate the constitution of that society, must be in unstable equilibrium. A small touch will overthrow it, and scarcely any human power will re-establish it. And this is the necessary effect of capitalistic slavery, for it prevents all other labourers, makes slaves the 'many' of the community, and fills their mind with grief and hatred. Capitalistic slavery is, as history shows, one of the easiest things to efface, as domestic slavery is one of the hardest. But capitalistic slavery has vitally influenced most of the greatest civilisations; and as domestic slavery has influenced nearly all of them, the entire effect of the two has been prodigious.

We see then that there are at least four conditions to be satisfied before this axiom of our English Political Economy is true within a nation. Before labour can move easily and as it pleases from employment to employment there must be such employments for it to move between ;—there must be an effectual Government capable of maintaining peace and order during the transition, and not requiring itself to be supported by fixity of station in society as so many governments have been ;—the nation must be capable of maintaining its independent existence against other nations without a military system dependent on localised and immovable persons ; and there must be no competing system of involuntary labour limiting the number of employments or moving between them more perfectly than contemporary free labour. These are not indeed all the conditions needful for the truth of the axiom, but the others can be explained better when some other matters have been first discussed.

II.

THE TRANSFERABILITY OF CAPITAL.

IN my last paper I discussed the fundamental principle of English Political Economy, that within the limits of a nation labour migrates from employment to employment, as increased remuneration attracts or decreased remuneration repels it; and now I have to treat the corresponding principle as to capital, that it flows or tends to flow to trades of which the profits are high, that it leaves or tends to leave those in which the profits are low, and that in consequence there is a tendency—a tendency limited and contracted, but still a tendency—to an equality of profits through commerce.

First, this requires such a development of the division of labour as to create what we call 'trade,' that is to say, a set of persons working for the wants of others, and providing for their own wants by the return-commodities received from those others. But this development has only been gradually acquired

F

by the human race. Captain Cook found some Australian tribes to whom the idea of traffic seemed unknown. They received what was given them readily, but they received it as a present only; they seemed to have no notion of giving anything in lieu of it. The idea of barter—an idea usually so familiar to the lower races of men—appeared never to have dawned on these very low ones. But among races in such a condition there is no change of trades as capital becomes more and more profitable in any one. The very conception comes long after. Every-one works for himself at everything; and he always works most at what he likes most for the time; as he changes his desires, so far as he can he changes his labour. Whenever he works he uses the few tools he has, the stone implements, the charred wood, the thongs of hide, and other such things, in the best way he can; a hundred savages are doing so at once, some in one way, some in another, and these are no doubt 'shiftings of capital.' But there is no computation of profit, as we now reckon profit, on such shiftings. Profit, as we calculate, means that which is over after the capital is replaced. But a savage incapable of traffic does not make this calculation as to his flints and his hides. The idea could not even be explained to him.

Secondly, this comparison requires a medium in which the profits can be calculated, that is, a *money*. Supposing that in the flax trade profits are 5 per cent., and that side by side in the cotton trade they are 15 per cent., capital will now-a-days immediately run from one to the other. And it does so because those who are making much, try to get more capital, and those who are making little—still more those who are losing—do not care to keep as much as they have. But if there is no money to compute in, neither will know what they are making, and therefore the process of migration wants its motive, and will not begin. The first sign of extra profit in a trade—not a conclusive, but a strongly presumptive one—is an extra high price in the article that trade makes or sells; but this test fails altogether when there is no 'money' to sell in. And the debit side of the account, the cost of production, is as difficult to calculate when there is no common measure between its items, or between the product, and any of them. Political Economists have indeed an idea of 'exchangeable value'—that is, of the number of things which each article will exchange for—and they sometimes suppose a state of barter in which people had this notion, and in which they calculated the profit of a trade by deducting the exchangeable

value of the labour and commodities used in its production from the value of the finished work. But
such a state of society never existed in reality. No
nation which was not clever enough to invent a
money, was ever able to conceive so thin and hard
an idea as 'exchangeable value.' Even now Mr.
Fawcett justly says that it puzzles many people, and
sends them away frightened from books on Political
Economy. In fact it is an ideal which those used to
money prices have framed to themselves. They see
that the price of anything, the money it fetches, is
equal to its ' purchasing power' over things, and by
steadily attending they come to be able to think of
this ' purchasing power' separately, and to call and
reason upon it as exchangeable value. But the idea
is very treacherous even to skilled minds, and even
now-a-days not the tenth part of any population could
ever take it in. As for the nations really in a state
of barter ever comprehending it, no one can imagine
it, for they are mostly unequal to easy arithmetic,
and some cannot count five. A most acute traveller
thus describes the actual process of bargaining among
savage nations as he saw it. 'In practice,' Mr.
Galton tells us of the Damaras, ' whatever they may
possess in their language, they certainly use no
numeral greater than three. When they wish to

express four they take to their fingers, which are to them as formidable instruments of calculation as a sliding rule is to an English schoolboy. They puzzle very much after five, because no spare hand remains to grasp and secure the fingers that are required for "units." Yet they seldom lose oxen : the way in which they discover the loss of one is not by the number of the herd being diminished, but by the absence of a face which they know. When bartering is going on each sheep must be paid for separately. Thus suppose two sticks of tobacco to be the rate of exchange for one sheep, it would sorely puzzle a Damara to take two sheep and give him four sticks. I have done so, and seen a man first put two of the sticks apart, and take a sight over them at one of the sheep he was about to sell. Having satisfied himself that that one was honestly paid for, and finding to his surprise that exactly two sticks remained in hand to settle the account for the other sheep, he would be afflicted with doubts; the transaction seemed too pat to be correct, and he would refer back to the first couple of sticks, and then his mind got hazy and confused, and wandered from one sheep to the other, and he broke off the transaction until two sticks were put into his hand and one sheep driven away, and then the other two sticks

given him, and the second sheep driven away.' Such
a delineation of primitive business speaks for itself,
and it is waste of space showing further that an
abstraction like 'value in exchange' is utterly beyond
the reach of the real bartering peoples—that a habit
of using money, and of computing in it, are necessary
preliminaries to comparisons of profits.

Unquestionably the most primitive community
can see if a pursuit utterly fails, or if it immensely
succeeds. The earliest men must have been eager in
making flint tools, for there are so many of them, and
no doubt they did not try to breed cattle where they
died. But there was in those days no adjusted comparison between one thing and another ; all pursuits
which anyhow suited went on then as they do among
savages now.

Money, too, is in this matter essential, or all but
essential, in another way. It is a form in which
capital is held *in suspense* without loss. The transfer
of capital from employment to employment is a matter
requiring consideration, consideration takes time, and
the capital must be somewhere during that time.
But most articles are bought at a risk ; they lose in
the process, and become second-hand ; an ordinary
person cannot get rid of them without receiving for
them less—often much less—than he gave. But

money is never 'second-hand;' it will always fetch itself, and it loses nothing by keeping. No doubt modern civilisation has invented some other forms of property which are almost as good to hold as money. Some interest-bearing securities, like Exchequer bills, are so, and pay an interest besides. But these are the creatures of money, so to say, and based upon it; they presuppose it, and would not be possible without it. A community of pure barter, even if it could reckon and compare profits, would not be able to move capital accurately from one trade to another, for it possesses no commodity which could, without risk of loss that could not be calculated, be held idle during the computation.

The refined means by which the movement is now effected is one of the nicest marvels of our commercial civilisation. The three principal of them are as follows:—

First,—There is the whole of the loan fund of the country lying in the hands of bankers and bill-brokers, which moves in an instant towards a trade that is unusually profitable, if only that trade can pro duce securities which come within banking rules. Supposing the corn trade to become particularly good, there are immediately twice the usual number of corn bills in the bill-brokers' cases; and if the iron trade,

then of iron bills. You could almost see the change
of capital, if you could look into the bill cases at different
times. But what you could not see is the
mental skill and knowledge which have made that
transfer, and without which it could not have been
made safely. Probably it would be new to many
people if stated plainly; but a very great many of the
strongest heads in England spend their minds on little
else than on thinking whether other people will pay
their debts. The life of Lombard Street bill-brokers
is almost exclusively so spent. Mr. Chapman, one of
the partners in Overend, Gurney, and Co., once rather
amused a parliamentary committee by speaking with
unction and enthusiasm of ' paper of the very finest
quality,' by which he meant paper on which the best
promises were written. Bills of exchange are only
undertakings to pay money, and the most likely to be
paid are, in the market phrase, of the ' finest quality,'
and the less likely of inferior quality. The mind of
a man like Mr. Chapman, if it could be looked into,
would be found to be a graduating machine marking
in an instant the rises and falls of pecuniary likeli-
hood. Each banker in his own neighbourhood is the
same; he is a kind of ' solvency-meter,' and lives by
estimating rightly the 'responsibility of parties,' as
he would call it. And the only reason why the

London bill-broker has to do it on a greater scale is that, being in the great centre, he receives the surplus savings not of one district but of many, which find no means of employment there. He is thus become the greatest and most just measurer of moneyed means and moneyed probity which the world has ever seen ;—to reduce it to its lowest terms, he knows that more people will pay more debts than anyone who now is, or ever before was, in the world. And the combined aggregate of these persons is a prepared machine ready to carry capital in any direction. The moment any set of traders want capital, the best of them, those whose promises are well known to be good, get it in a minute, because it is lying ready in the hands of those who know, and who live by knowing, that they are fit to have it.

Secondly,—In modern England, there is a great speculative fund which is always ready to go into anything which promises high profits. The largest part of this is composed of the savings of men of business. When, as in 1871, the profits of many trades suddenly become much greater than usual, the Stock Exchange instantly becomes animated ; there is at once a market for all kinds of securities, so long as they promise much, either by great interest or by rise of prices. Men of business who are used to a high

percentage of profit in their own trade despise 3 or 4
per cent., and think that they ought to have much
more. In consequence there is no money so often
lost as theirs ; there is an idea that it is the country
clergyman and the ignorant widow who mostly lose
by bad loans and bad companies. And no doubt they
often do lose. But I believe that it is oftener still
men of business, of slight education and of active
temperament, who have made money rapidly, and
who fancy that the skill and knowledge of a special
trade which have enabled them to do so, will also
enable them to judge of risks, and measure con-
tingencies out of that trade ; whereas, in fact, there
are no persons more incompetent, for they think they
know everything, when they really know almost
nothing out of their little business, and by habit and
nature they are eager to be doing. So much of their
money as comes to London is in greater jeopardy
almost than any other money. But there is a great
deal which never comes there, and which those who
make it are able to put out in pushing their own trade
and in extending allied trades. The very defects
which make the trader so bad a judge of other things
make him an excellent judge of these, and he is ready
and daring, and most quick to make use of what he
knows. Each trade in modern commerce is surrounded

by subsidiary and kindred trades, which familiarise
the imagination with it, and make its state known;
as soon, therefore, as the conspicuous dealers in that
trade are known to be doing particularly well, the
people in the surrounding trades say, ' Why should
not we do as well too ?' and they embark their capital
in it—sometimes, of course, wrongly, but upon the
whole wisely and beneficially. In an animated business world like ours, these inroads into the trades
with largest gains by the nearest parts of the speculative fund are incessant, and are a main means of
equalising profits.

Lastly,—There is the obvious tendency of young
men starting in business to go into the best-paying
business, or what is thought to be so at that time.
This, in the best cases, also acts mainly on the allied
and analogous trades. Little good, for the most
part, comes of persons who have been brought up on
one side of the business world going quite to the
other side—of farmers' sons going to cotton-spinning,
or of lacemakers' sons going into shipping. Each
sort of trade has a tradition of its own, which is
never written, probably could not be written, which
can only be learned in fragments, and which is best
taken in early life, before the mind is shaped and the
ideas fixed. From all surrounding trades there is an

incessant movement of young men with new money
into very profitable trades, which steadily tends to
reduce that profitableness to the common average.

I am more careful than might seem necessary to
describe the entire process of equalisation at length,
because it is only by so doing that we can see how
complex it is, and how much development in society
it requires; but as yet the description is not complete, or nearly so. We have only got as far as the
influx of money into new trades, but this is but a
small part of what is necessary. Trades do not live
by money alone; money by itself will not make anything. What, then, do we mean when we speak of
'capital' as flowing from employment to employment?

Some writers speak as if the only thing which
transfers of capital effect is a change in the sort of
labour that is set in motion; and no doubt this is
so far true, that all new employments of capital do
require new labour. Human labour is the primitive
moving force, and you must have more of it if you
want more things done; but the description, though
true, is most incomplete, as the most obvious facts
in the matter prove. When new capital comes into
cotton-spinning, this means not only that new money
is applied to paying cotton operatives, but also that

new money is applied to buying new spinning
machines; these spinning machines are made by
other machines, as well as labour; and the second lot
of machines again by a third set, as well as other
labour. In the present state of the world, nothing
is made by brute labour; everything is made by aids
to labour; and when capital goes from trade to
trade, it settles not only which sort of labour shall
be employed, but which sort of existing machines
should be first used up, which sort of new ones
made, and how soon those new ones shall be worn
out, not only in the selected trade, but in an endless
series subsidiary to it.

To understand the matter fully, we must have a
distinct view of what on this occasion and on this
matter we mean by 'capital.' The necessity of a
science like Political Economy is that it must borrow
its words from common life, and therefore from a
source where they are not used accurately, and cannot be used accurately. When we come to reason
strictly on the subjects to which they relate, we must
always look somewhat precisely to their meaning;
and the worst is that it will not do, if you are writing for the mass of men, even of educated men, to
use words always in the same sense. Common words
are so few, that if you tie them down to one meaning

they are not enough for your purpose; they do their
work in common life because they are in a state
of incessant slight variation, meaning one thing in
one discussion and another a little different in the
next. If we were really to write an invariable
nomenclature in a science where we have so much
to say of so many things as we have in Political
Economy, we must invent new terms, like the
writers on other sciences. Mr. De Morgan said (in
defence of some fresh-coined substantive), 'Mathematics must not want words because Cicero did not
know the differential calculus.' But a writer on
Political Economy is bound—not perhaps by Cicero
—but by his readers. He must not use words out
of his own head, which they never heard of; they
will not read him if he does. The best way, as we
cannot do this, is to give up uniform uses—to write
more as we do in common life, where the context is a
sort of unexpressed 'interpretation clause,' showing
in what sense words are used; only, as in Political
Economy we have more difficult things to speak of
than in common conversation, we must take more
care, give more warning of any change, and at
times write out the 'interpretation clause' for that
page or discussion, lest there should be any mistake.
I know that this is difficult and delicate work;

and all I have to say in defence of it is that in practice it is safer than the competing plan of inflexible definitions. Anyone who tries to express varied meanings on complex things with a scanty vocabulary of fastened senses, will find that his style grows cumbrous without being accurate, that he has to use long periphrases for common thoughts, and that after all he does not come out right, for he is half his time falling back into the senses which fit the case in hand best, and these are sometimes one, sometimes another, and almost always different from his ' hard and fast ' sense. In such discussions we should learn to vary our definitions as we want, just as we say, ' let x, y, z mean ' now this, and now that, in different problems; and this, though they do not always avow it, is really the practice of the clearest and most effective writers.

By capital, then, in this discussion, we mean an aggregate of two unlike sorts of artificial commodities —co-operative things which help labour, and re-munerative things which pay for it. The two have this in common, that they are the produce of human labour, but they differ in almost everything else if you judge of them by the visual appearance. Between a loaf of bread and a steam-engine, between a gimlet and a piece of bacon, there looks as if there were really

nothing in common, except that man manufactured
both. But, though the contrast of externalities is so
great, the two have a most essential common property which is that which Political Economy fixes
upon ; the possible effect of both is to augment
human wealth. Labourers work because they want
bread ; their work goes farther if they have good tools ;
and therefore economists have a common word for
both tools and bread. They are both capital, and
other similar things are so too.

And here we come across another of the inevitable verbal difficulties of Political Economy. Taking
its words from common life, it finds that at times
and for particular discussions it must twist them in
a way which common people would never think of.
The obvious resemblances which we deal with in life
dictate one mode of grouping objects in the mind,
and one mode of speaking of them ; the latent but
more powerful resemblance which science finds would
dictate another form of speech and mental grouping.
And then what seems a perverse use of language
must be made. Thus, for the present discussion, the
acquired skill of a labourer is capital, though no one
in common life would call it so. It is a productive
thing made by man, as much as any tool; it *is*, in
fact, an immaterial tool which the labourer uses just

as he does a material one. It is co-operative capital as much as anything can be. And then, again, the most unlikely-looking and luxurious articles are capital if they reward and stimulate labour. Artisans like the best of rabbits, the best bits of meat, green peas, and gin; they work to get these; they would stay idle if they were not incited by these, and therefore these are 'capital.' Political Economy (like most moral sciences) requires not only to change its definitions as it moves from problem to problem, but also for some problems to use definitions which, unless we see the motive, seem most strange; just as in Acts of Parliament the necessity of the draftsman makes a very technical use of words necessary if he is to do his work neatly, and the reader will easily be most mistaken and confused if he does not heed the dictionary which such Acts contain.

Remembering all this, we see at once that it is principally remunerative capital which is transferable from employment to employment. Some tools and instruments are, no doubt, used in many trades, especially the complex ones; knives, hammers, twine, and nails can be used, are used, in a thousand. The existing stock of these is transferred bodily when capital migrates from an employment.

But, in general, as I have said before, the effect of the migration on co-operative capital is to change the speed with which the existing machines are worked out, and the nature of the new machines which are made; the 'live skill' of an artisan being treated as a machine. On remunerative capital the effect is simpler. As a rule, much the same commodities reward labour in different trades, and if one trade declines and another rises, the only effect is to change the labourer who gets these commodities; or, if the change be from a trade which employs little skilled labour to one which employs much, then the costly commodities which skilled labour wants will be in demand, more of them will be made, and there will be an increase of animation in all the ancillary trades which help their making.

We see also more distinctly than before what we mean by an 'employment.' We mean a group of persons with fitting tools and of fitting skill paid by the things they like. I purposely speak of 'tools' to include all machines, even the greatest, for I want to fix attention on the fact that everything depends on the effort of man,—on the primary fruit of human labour. Without this to start with, all else is useless. And I use it out of brevity to include such things as coal and materials, which for any other purpose no one would call so, but which are plainly the same for what we have now to do with.

And 'employment' in any large trade implies an 'employer.' The capitalist is the motive power in modern production, in the 'great commerce.' He settles what goods shall be made, and what not; what brought to market, and what not. He is the general of the army; he fixes on the plan of operations, organises its means, and superintends its execution. If he does this well, the business succeeds and continues; if he does it ill, the business fails and ceases. Everything depends on the correctness of the unseen decisions, on the secret sagacity of the determining mind. And I am careful to dwell on this, though it is so obvious, and though no man of business would think it worth mentioning, because books forget it,—because the writers of books are not familiar with it. They are taken with the conspicuousness of the working classes; they hear them say, it is we who made Birmingham, we who made Manchester, but you might as well say that it was the 'compositors' who made the 'Times' newspaper. No doubt the craftsmen were necessary to both, but of themselves they were insufficient to either. The printers do not settle what is to be printed; the writers even do not

settle what is to be written. It is the editor who
settles everything. He creates the 'Times' from
day to day; on his power of hitting the public fancy
its prosperity and power rest; everything depends
on his daily bringing to the public exactly what the
public wants to buy; the rest of Printing-House
Square—all the steam-presses, all the type, all the
staff, clever as so many of them are,—are but implements which he moves. In the very same way the
capitalist edits the 'business;' it is he who settles
what commodities to offer to the public; how and
when to offer them, and all the rest of what is
material. This monarchical structure of money
business increases as society goes on, just as the
corresponding structure of war business does, and
from the same causes. In primitive times a battle
depends as much on the prowess of the best fighting
men, of some Hector or some Achilles, as on the
good science of the general. But now-a-days it is a
man at the far end of a telegraph wire—a Count
Moltke, with his head over some papers,—who sees
that the proper persons are slain, and who secures
the victory. So in commerce. The primitive
weavers are separate men with looms apiece, the
primitive weapon-makers separate men with flints
apiece; there is no organised action, no planning,

contriving, or foreseeing in either trade, except on the smallest scale ; but now the whole is an affair of money and management ; of a thinking man in a dark office, computing the prices of guns or worsteds. No doubt in some simple trades these essential calculations can be verified by several persons—by a board of directors, or something like it. But these trades, as the sagacity of Adam Smith predicted, and as painful experience now shows, are very few ; the moment there comes anything difficult or complicated, the Board 'does not see its way,' and then, except it is protected by a monopoly, or something akin to monopoly, the individual capitalist beats it out of the field. But the details of this are not to my present purpose. The sole point now material is that the transference of capital from employment to employment involves the pre-existence of employment, and this pre-existence involves that of 'employers :' of a set of persons—one or many, though usually one—who can effect the transfer of that capital from employment to employment, and can manage it when it arrives at the employment to which it is taken.

And this management implies knowledge. In all cases successful production implies the power of adapting means to ends, of making what you want as you want it. But after the division of labour has arisen, it implies much more than this : it then requires, too, that the producer should know the wants of the consumer, a man whom mostly he has never seen, whose name probably he does not know, very likely even speaking another language, living according to other habits, and having scarcely any point of intimate relation to the producer, except a liking for what he produces. And if a person who does not see is to suit another who is not seen, he must have much head-knowledge,—an acquired learning in strange wants as well as of the mode of making things to meet them. A person possessing that knowledge is necessary to the process of transferring capital, for he alone can use it when the time comes, and if he is at the critical instant not to be found, the change fails, and the transfer is a loss and not a gain.

This description of the process by which capital is transferred and of what we mean by it, may seem long, but it will enable us to be much shorter in showing the conditions which that transfer implies. First, it presupposes the existence of transferable labour, and I showed before how rare transferable labour is in the world, and how very peculiar are its prerequisites. You cannot have it unless you have a strong government, which will keep peace in the delicate line on which people are moving. You must not have fixed castes in inherited occupations, which at first are ways and means to do without a strong government, but which often last on after it begins; you must not have a local army which roots men to. fixed spots for military purposes, and therefore very much to fixed pursuits; and you must not have slavery, for this is an imperfect substitute for free transferable labour, which effectually prevents the existence of it. Complete freedom of capital pre-supposes complete freedom of labour, and can only be attained when and where this exists.

No doubt capital begins to move much before the movement of labour is perfect. The first great start of it commences with a very unpopular person, who is almost always spoken evil of when his name is mentioned, but in whom those who know the great things of which he has been the forerunner will always take a great interest. It is the money-lender in a primitive community, whose capital is first transferred readily from occupation to occupation. Suppose a new crop, say cotton, becomes suddenly lucrative, immediately the little proprietors throng to the money-lenders to obtain funds to buy cotton. A new trade is begun by his help, which could not have been begun without him. If cotton ceases to be a good crop, he ceases to lend to grow it, his spare capital either remains idle or goes to some other loan,—perhaps to help some other crop which has taken the place of cotton in profitableness. There is no more useful trade in early civilisation, though there is none which has such a bad name, and not unnaturally, for there is none which then produces more evil as well as good. Securities for loans, such as we have them in developed commerce, are rarely to be met with in early times; the land— the best security as we think it—is then mostly held upon conditions which prevent its being made in that way available; there is little movable property of much value, and peasants who work the land have scarcely any of that little; the only thing they can really pledge is their labour—*themselves*. But then when the loan is not paid, 'realising the security' is only possible by making the debtor a slave, and as this is very painful, the creditor who makes much use of it is hated. Even when the land can be pledged, peasant proprietors never think that it ought really to be taken if the debt for which it is pledged is not paid. They think that the land is still theirs, no matter how much has been lent them upon it, or how much they have neglected to pay.

But odious as the ' usurer ' thus becomes, he is most useful really, and the beginner of the movement which creates the ' great commerce.'

Another condition which precedes the free transfer of labour—the first prerequisite of the free transfer of capital—is slavery, and within its limits this is free enough; indeed, more free than anything else similar, for you have not to consult the labourer at all, as in all other organisations you must. The capitalist buys the slave and sets him to do, not what the slave likes, but what he himself likes. I can imagine that a theorist would say beforehand that this was the best way of getting things done, though not for the happiness of the doer. It makes the ' working group' into an army where the general is absolute, and desertion penal. But so subtle is the nature of things, that actual trial shows this structure of society not to be industrially superior to all others, but to be very ineffectual indeed, and industrially inferior to most of them. The slave will not work except he is made, and therefore he does little; he is none the better, or little the better, if he does his work well than if he does it ill, and therefore he rarely cares to do it very well. On a small scale, and under careful supervision, a few slaves carefully trained may be made to do very good work, but on

any large scale it is impossible. A gang of slaves
can do nothing but what is most simple and easy,
and most capable of being looked after. The South-
ern States of America, for some years before their
rebellion, were engaged in trying on the greatest
scale and the most ample means the world has ever
seen the experiment how far slavery would go ; and
the result is easily stated ; they never could ' make
brute force go beyond brute work.'

Next, in order that capital can be transferred, it
must exist and be at the disposal of persons who
wish to transfer it. This is especially evident as to
remunerative capital, which we have seen to be the
most transferable of all capital. But the earliest
wages-paying commodities—the food and the neces-
saries which in simple communities the labourer
desires—are accumulated by persons who want them
for their own use, and who will not part with them.
The ' untransferable ' labourer—the labourer confined
to a single occupation in a primitive society—saves
certain things for himself, and needs them for himself,
but he has no extra stock. He has no use, indeed,
for it. In a society where there is no transferable
labour, or need to hire, there is no motive, or almost
none, for an accumulation of wages-paying capital
which is to buy labour. The idea of it, simple as it

seems to us, is one of a much later age, like that in which labour seeking to be hired is the commonest of things, and therefore the commodities needed for hiring it are among the commonest too. The means of buying, and the thing bought, inevitably in such a case as this grow together.

As to the other kind of capital—that which aids labour, the co-operative kind—the scientific study of savage tribes, which is so peculiar a feature of the present world, has brought out its scantiness—I might say its meanness—almost more distinctly than it has brought out anything else. Sir John Lubbock, one of our greatest instructors on this matter, tells us the implements of the Australians are very simple. ' They have no knowledge of pottery, and carry water in skins, or in vessels made of bark. They are quite ignorant of warm water, which strikes them with great amazement.' Some of them carry ' a small bag about the size of a moderate cabbage net, which is made by laying threads, loop within loop, somewhat in the manner of knitting used by our ladies to make purses. This bag the man carries loose upon his back by a small string, which passes over his head ; it generally contains a lump or two of paint and resin, some fish-hooks and lines, a shell or two out of which these hooks are made, a few points of darts, and their

usual ornaments, which include the whole worldly
treasure of the richest man among them.' All
travellers say that rude nations have no *stock* of
anything—no materials lying ready to be worked
up, no idle tools waiting to be used ; the whole is a
' hand-to-mouth' world. And this is but another way
of saying that in such societies there is no capital of
this kind to be transferred. We said just now that
what we meant by transfer in such a case was a
change in the sort of stock—the kind of materials,
the kind of machines, the kind of living things to be
used fastest and worn out quickest. But in these
poverty-stricken early societies there is substantially
no such stock at all. Every petty thing which there
exists is already being used for all its petty purposes,
and cannot be worked more quickly than it already
is, or be worn out more rapidly than it is being worn
out.

Next, this capital must be concentrated in ' trades,'
else it cannot be transferred from trade to trade for
the sake of profit, and it must be worked by a single
capitalist, or little group of capitalists, as the case
may be, else the trade will not yield profit. And
this, as has been explained, is not a universal feature
of all times, but a special characteristic of somewhat
advanced eras. And there must be the knowledge

capable of employing that capital—a knowledge which altogether differs in different trades. Now-a-days the amount of the difference is a little disguised from us because we see people with 'capital' in various pursuits—that is, who are traders in each and all of them. But such persons could not do this unless they were assisted by more specialised persons. The same principle governs political administration. Sir George Lewis, one of the most capable judges of it in our time, has observed—' The permanent officers of a department are the depositaries of its official tradition ; they are generally referred to by the political head of the office for information on questions of official practice, and knowledge of this sort acquired in one department would be useless in another. If, for example, the chief clerk of the criminal department of the Home Office were to be transferred to the Foreign Office, or to the Admiralty, the special experience which he has acquired at the Home Office, and which is in daily requisition for the guidance of the Home Secretary, would be utterly valueless to the Foreign Secretary, or to the First Lord of the Admiralty. . . . Where a general superintendence is required, and assistance can be obtained from subordinates, and where the chief qualifications are judgment, sagacity, and enlightened political opinions,

such a change of offices is possible; but as you
descend lower in the official scale, the speciality of
functions increases. The duties must be performed
in person, with little or no assistance, and there is
consequently a necessity for special knowledge and
experience. Hence the same person may be successively at the head of the Home Office, the Foreign
Office, the Colonial Office, and the Admiralty; he
may be successively President of the Board of Trade,
and Chancellor of the Exchequer; but to transfer an
experienced clerk from one office to another would be
like transferring a skilful naval officer to the army, or
appointing a military engineer officer to command a
ship of war.' And just so in mercantile business—
there are certain general principles which are common
to all kinds of it, and a person can be of considerable
use in more than one kind if he understands these
principles, and has the proper sort of mind. But the
appearance of this common element is in commerce,
as in politics, a sign of magnitude, and primitive
commerce is all petty. In early tribes there is
nothing but the special man—the clothier, the mason,
the weapon-maker. Each craft tried to be, and very
much was, a mystery except to those who carried it
on. The knowledge required for each was possessed
by few, kept secret by those few, and nothing else

was of use but this monopolised and often inherited acquirement; there was no 'general' business knowledge. The idea of a general art of money-making is very modern; almost everything ancient about it is individual and particular. Distance helped much in this kind of speciality. 'To the great fair of Stourbridge,' in the south of England, there came, we are told, besides foreign products, 'the woolpacks, which then formed the riches of England, and were the envy of outer nations. The Cornish tin-mine sent its produce, stamped with the sign of the rich earl who bought the throne of the German Empire, or of the warlike prince who had won his spurs at Crecy, and captured the French king at Poitiers. . . . Thither came also salt from the springs of Worcestershire, as well as that which had been gathered under the summer sun from the salterns of the eastern coasts. Here, too, might be found lead from the mines of Derbyshire, and iron, either raw or manufactured, from the Sussex forges.' In an age when locomotion was tedious and costly, the mere distance of the separate seats of industry tended to make separate monopolies of them. Other difficulties of transferring capital were aggravated by the rarity and the localisation of the knowledge necessary for carrying it on.

Next, as we have seen, for the attraction of capital from trade to trade, there must be a money in which to calculate such profits, and a good money too. Many media of interchange which have been widely used in the world, and which are quite good enough for many purposes, are quite unfit for this. Cattle, for instance, which were certainly one of the first-used kinds of money, and which have been said to have been that most used, because what we call the primitive ages lasted so long, are quite inadequate. They are good enough for present bargains, but not for the forward and backward-looking calculations of profit and loss. The notation is not distinct enough for accuracy. One cow is not exactly like another; a price list saying that so much raw cotton was worth 20 cows, and so much cotton worth 30 cows, would not tell much for the purpose; you could not be sure what cows you would have to give or you would get. There might be a 'loss by exchange' which would annihilate profit. Until you get good coined money, calculations of profit and loss that could guide capital are impossible.

Next, there must be the means of shifting 'money,' which we analysed—the loan fund, the speculative fund, and the choice of employment by young capitalists, or some of them. The loan fund on a small scale is, as we have seen, a very early institution; it begins in the primitive village almost as soon as any kind of trade begins at all, and a perception of its enormous value is one of the earliest pieces of true economical speculation. 'In the Athenian laws,' says Demosthenes, 'are many well-devised securities for the protection of the creditor; for commerce proceeds not from the borrowers, but from the lenders, without whom no vessel, no navigator, no traveller could depart from port.' Even in these days we could hardly put the value of discounts and trade loans higher. But though the loan fund begins so early in civilisation, and is prized so soon, it grows very slowly; the full development, modern banking such as we are familiar with in England, stops where the English language ceases to be spoken. The peculiarity of that system is that it utilises all the petty cash of private persons down nearly to the end of the middle class. This is lodged with bankers on running account, and though incessantly changing in distribution, the quantity is nearly fixed on the whole, for most of what one person pays out others almost directly pay in; and therefore it is so much added to the loan fund which bankers have to use, though, as credit is always precarious, they can, of course, only use it with caution. Besides this,

H

English bankers have most of the permanent savings of little persons deposited with them, and so have an unexampled power of ready lending. But ages of diffused confidence are necessary to establish such a system, and peculiar circumstances in the banking history of England, and of Scotland still more, have favoured it. Our insular position exempting us from war, and enabling our free institutions to develop both quietly and effectually, is at the very root of it. But here until within a hundred years there was no such concentration of minute moneys, no such increment to the loan fund, and abroad there is nothing equal to it now. Taking history as a whole, it is a rare and special phenomenon. Mostly the loan fund of a country consists of such parts of its moneyed savings as those who have saved them are able to lend for themselves. As countries advance banking slowly begins, and some persons who are believed to have much, are entrusted with the money of others, and become a sort of middlemen to put it out; but almost everywhere the loan fund is very small to our English notions. It is a far less efficient instrument for conveying capital from trade to trade everywhere else than here; in very many countries it is only incipient; in some it can hardly be said to exist at all.

The speculative fund, as I have called it, has also

but a bounded range of action. The number of persons who have large moneyed savings who are willing to invest them in new things is in England considerable, but in most countries it is small. Such persons fear the unknown; they have a good deal to lose, and they do not wish to lose it. In most communities there is not even the beginning of a settled opinion to tell them which undertaking is likely to be good, and which bad. In the industrial history of most countries, the most marked feature is an extreme monotony; enterprises are few; the same things continue for ages to be done in the same way. The *data* which should guide original minds are few and insufficient; there was not such a thing as a 'price list' in any ancient community. No Athenian merchant could, by looking over a file of figures, see which commodities were much lower in their average price, and which therefore might be advantageously bought with money that he could not employ in his usual trade. Even for so simple a speculation as this, according to our present notions, the *data* did not exist, and for more complex ones the knowledge was either altogether wanting or confined to a few persons, none of whom might have the idle capital. The speculative fund does not become a force of first-rate magnitude till we have in the same community a great accumulation of spare capital, and a wide diffusion of sound trade knowledge,—and then it does.

The free choice by young men of the mode in which they will invest the capital which they possess is also in the early times of trade much hindered and cramped, and it only gains anything near the effective influence which it now has with us in quite late times. For a long period of industrial history special associations called ‘guilds’ prohibited it; these kept each trade apart, and prevented capital from going from one to the other. They even kept the trade of city A quite apart from the same trade in city B; they would not let capital or labour flow from one to the other. These restrictive hedges grew up naturally, and there was no great movement to throw them down. They strengthened what was already strong, and that which was weak made no protest. The general ignorance of trade matters in such communities made it seem quite reasonable to keep each trade to those who understood it; other people going into it would, it was imagined, only do it ill, lose their money, and hurt those who did it well by a pernicious competition. We now know that this is a great error, that such guilds did far more harm than good, that only experiment can show where capital will answer in trade, that it is from the outsider that the best improvements commonly come. But these things, which are now commonplaces after experience, were paradoxes before it. The first deduction of the uninstructed mind was and is the other way. Nor is it dispelled by mere argument. Civilisation must increase, trade ideas must grow and spread, and idle capital waiting to change must accumulate. Till these things have happened, the free choice by a young man how he will invest his capital is not the common rule, but the rare exception; it is not what mostly happens, though it may be resisted, but what happens only where it is unusually helped. Even where there is no formal guild, the circumstances which have elsewhere created so many, create an informal monopoly, mostly much stronger than any force which strives to infringe it.

None, therefore, of the three instruments which now convey capital from employment to employment can in early times be relied on for doing so, even when that capital exists, and when some labour at least is available to be employed by it; neither the loan fund, nor the speculative fund, nor the free choice of a trade by young men, is then a commonly predominant power; nor do the whole three taken together commonly come to much in comparison with the forces opposed to them.

And even if their intrinsic strength had been far greater than it was, it would often have been successfully impeded by the want of a final condition to the free transfer of capital, of which I have not spoken yet. This is a political condition. We have seen that for the free transfer of labour from employment to employment a strong government is necessary. The rules regulating the inheritance of trades and the fixed separations of labour were really contrivances to obtain some part of the results of the division of labour, when for want of an effectual government, punishing quarrels and preserving life, free competition and movement in labour were impossible. And this same effectual government is equally necessary, as need not be explained, for the free migration of money. That migration needs peace and order quite as obviously as the migration of labour; and those who understand the delicacy of the process will need no proof of it. But though a strong government is required, something more is wanted too; for the movement of capital we need a *fair* government. If capital is to be tempted from trade to trade by the prospect of high profits, it must be allowed to keep those profits when they have been made. But the primitive notion of taxation is that when a government sees much money it should take some of it, and that if it sees more money it should take more of it. Adam Smith laid down, as a fundamental canon, that taxes ought to be levied at the time when, and in the manner in which, it is most easy for the taxpayer to pay them. But the primitive rule is to take them when and how it is most easy to find and seize them. Under governments with that rule persons who are doing well shrink from showing that they are doing well; those who are making money refuse to enjoy themselves, and will show none of the natural signs of that money, lest the tax-gatherer should appear and should take as much as he likes of it. A socialist speaker once spoke of a 'healthy habit of confiscation,' and that habit has been much diffused over the world. Wherever it exists it is sure exceedingly to impede the movements of capital, and where it abounds to prevent them.

These reasonings give us a conception of a 'pre-economic' era when the fundamental postulates of Political Economy, of which we have spoken, were not realised, and show us that the beginnings of all wealth were made in that era. Primitive capital accumulated in the hands of men who could neither move it nor themselves—who really never thought of doing either—to whom either would often have seemed monstrous if they could have thought of it, and in whose case either was still more often prevented by insuperable difficulties. And this should warn us not to trust the historical retrospect of economists, merely because we see and know that their reasonings on the events and causes of the present world are right. Early times had different events and different causes. Reasoners like economists, and there are many others like them, are apt to modify the famous saying of Plunket; they turn history not into an old almanac, but into a new one. They make what happens now to have happened always, according to the same course of time.

And these reasonings also enable us to explain what is so common in all writing concerning those early and pre-economic times. One of the commonest phenomena of primitive trade is 'fixed' prices, and the natural inquiry of everyone who is trained in our Political Economy is, how could these prices be maintained? They seem impossible according to the teaching which he has received, and yet they were maintained for ages; they lasted longer than many things now-a-days which we do not reckon short-lived. One explanation is that they were maintained by custom; but this fails at the crisis, for the question is, how could the custom be maintained? The unchanging price could not always be right under changing circumstances. Why did not capital and labour flow into the trades which at the time had more than their 'natural' price, desert those which had less, and so disturb the first with a plethora, and the second with a scarcity? The answer we now see is that what we have been used to call 'natural' is not the first but the second nature of men ; that there were ages when capital and labour could not migrate, when trade was very much one of monopoly against monopoly. And in such a society, fixing a price is a primitive way of doing what in after ages we do as far as we can ; it is a mode of regulating the monopoly—of preventing the incessant dissensions which in all ages arise about what is a just price and what is not, when there is no competition to settle that price. The way in which 'custom' settles prices, how it gradually arrives at what is right and proper, or at least at what is endurable, one cannot well say ; probably many incipient customary prices break down before the one which suits and lasts is stumbled upon. But defects of this rule-of-thumb method are no reproach to primitive times. When we try to regulate monopolies ourselves we have arrived at nothing better. The fares of railways—the fixed prices at which these great monopolies carry passengers—are as accidental, as much the rough results of inconclusive experiments, as any prices can be.

And this long analysis proves so plainly, that it would be tedious to show it again, that the free movement of capital from employment to employment within a nation, and the consequent strong tendency to an equality of profits there, are ideals daily becoming truer as competition increases and capital grows, that all the hindrances are gradually diminishing, all the incentives enhancing, and all the instruments becoming keener, quicker, and more powerful.

But it is most important to observe that this ideal of English Political Economy is not like most of its ideals, an ultimate one. In fact the 'great commerce' has already gone beyond it; we can already distinctly foresee a time when that commerce will have merged it in something larger. English Political Economy, as we know, says that capital fluctuates from trade to trade within a nation, and it adds that capital will not as a rule migrate beyond that nation. 'Feelings,' says Ricardo, 'which I should be sorry to see weakened, induced most men of property to be satisfied with a low rate of profits in their own country, rather than seek a more advantageous employment for their wealth in foreign nations.' But these feelings are being weakened every day. A class of cosmopolitan capitalists has grown up which scarcely feels them at all. When Ricardo wrote, trade of the modern magnitude was new: long wars had separated most nations from most others, and especially had isolated England in habit and in feeling. Ricardo framed, and others have continued, a theory of foreign trade in which each nation is bounded by a ring-fence, through which capital cannot pass in or out. But the present state of things is far less simple, and much of that theory must be remodelled. The truth is that the three great instruments for transferring capital within a nation, whose operation we have analysed, have begun to operate on the largest scale between nations. The 'loan fund,' the first and most powerful of these, does so most strikingly. Whenever the English money market is bare of cash it can at once obtain it by raising the rate of interest. That is to say, it can borrow money to the extent of millions at any moment to meet its occasions: or what is the same thing, can call in loans of its own. Other nations can do so too, each in proportion to its credit and its wealth—though none so quickly as England,

on account of our superiority in these things. A
cosmopolitan loan fund exists, which runs everywhere as it is wanted, and as the rate of interest
tempts it.

A new commodity, one of the greatest growths
of recent times, is used to aid these operations. The
'securities' of all well-known countries, their national debts, their railway shares, and so on (a kind
of properties peculiar to the last two centuries, and
increasing now most rapidly), are dealt in through
Europe on every Stock Exchange. If the rate of
interest rises in any one country the price of such
securities falls; foreign countries come in and buy
them; they are sent abroad and their purchase-money
comes here. Such interest-bearing documents are
a sort of national 'notes of hand' which a country
puts out when it is poor, and buys back when it is
rich.

The mode in which the indemnity from France
to Germany was paid is the most striking instance
of this which ever occurred in the world. The sum
of 200,000,000*l.* was the largest ever paid by one
set of persons to another, upon a single contract,
since the system of payments began. Without a
great lending apparatus such an operation could not
have been effected. The resources of one nation, as

nations now are, would not have been equal to it. In fact it was the international loan fund which did the business. ' We may say,' M. Say states in his official report, ' that all the great banking-houses of Europe have concurred in this operation, and it is sufficient to show the extent and the magnitude of it to say that the number of houses which signed or concurred in the arrangement was fifty-five, and that many of them represented syndicates of bankers, so that the actual number concerned was far more considerable.' ' The concentration,' he adds, ' of the effects of all the banks of Europe produced results of an unhoped-for magnitude. All other business of a similar nature was almost suspended for a time, while the capital of all the private banks, and of all their friends, co-operated in the success of the French loans, and in the transmission of the money lent from country to country. This was a new fact in the economic history of Europe, and we should attach peculiar importance to it.' The magnitude of it as a single transaction was indeed very new ; but it is only a magnificent instance of what incessantly happens ; and the commonness of similar small transactions, and the amount of them when added together, are even more remarkable, and even more important than the size of this one ; and similar operations of the international 'loan fund' are going on constantly, though on a far less scale.

We must not, however, fancy that this puts all countries on a level, as far as capital is concerned, because it can be attracted from one to another. On the contrary, there will always tend to be a fixed difference between two kinds of countries. The old country, where capital accumulates, will always, on an average, have it cheaper than the new country, which has saved little, and can employ any quantity. The Americans in the Mississippi Valley are naturally a borrowing community, and the English at home are naturally lenders. And the rate of interest in the lending country will of course be less than that in the borrowing country. We see approaches—distant approaches even yet, but still distinct approaches— to a time at which all civilised and industrial countries will be able to obtain a proportionate share of the international loan fund, and will differ only in the rate they have to pay for it.

The 'speculative fund' is also becoming common to all countries, and it is the English who have taken the lead, because they have more money, more practical adaptation to circumstances, and more industrial courage than other nations. Some nations, no doubt, have as much or more of one of these

singly, but none have as much of the efficiency which
is the combined result of all three. The way in
which continental railways—the early ones especially, when the idea was novel—were made by English contractors is an example of this. When Mr.
Brassey, the greatest of them, was making the line
from Turin to Novara, for the Italian Government,
Count Cavour sent one morning for his agent, and
said, 'We are in a difficulty: the public have sub-
scribed for very few shares, but I am determined to
carry out the line, and I want to know if Mr.
Brassey will take half the deficiency if the Italian
Government will take the other half.' Mr. Brassey
did so, and thus the railway was made. This is the
international speculative fund in action, and the
world is filled with its triumphs.

So large, so daring, and indeed often so reckless
is this speculative fund, that some persons have imagined that there was nothing which would seem
absurd to it. A very little while ago, a scheme—a
fraudulent scheme, no doubt—was gravely brought
out, for a ship railway over the Isthmus of Panama ;
the ships were to be lifted upon the line on one side,
and lifted off and returned to the ocean on the other.
But even the 'speculative fund' would not stand that,
and the scheme collapsed. Yet the caricature shows

the reality; we may use it to remind ourselves how mobile this sort of money is, and how it runs from country to country like beads of quicksilver.

Young men also now transfer their capital from country to country with a rapidity formerly unknown. In Europe perhaps the Germans are most eminent in so doing. Their better school education, their better-trained habits of learning modern languages, and their readiness to bear the many privations of a residence among foreigners, have gained them a prominence certainly over the English and the French, perhaps above all other nations. But taking the world as a whole the English have a vast superiority. They have more capital to transfer, and their language is the language of 'the great commerce' everywhere, and tends to become so more and more. More transactions of the 'cosmopolitan speculative fund' are arranged in English, probably, than in all the other languages of the world put together; not only because of the wealth and influence of mere England, though that is not small, but because of the wealth and influence of the other States which speak that language also, the United States, our colonies, and British India, which uses it mostly for its largest trade. The number of English commercial houses all over the world is immense, and of American very many, and yearly a vast number of young Englishmen are sent out to join them. The pay is high, the prospect good, and insular as we are thought to be (and in some respects we are so most mischievously), the emigration of young men with English capital, and to manage English capital, is one of the great instruments of world-wide trade and one of the binding forces of the future.

In this way the same instruments which diffused capital through a nation are gradually diffusing it among nations. And the effect of this will be in the end much to simplify the problems of international trade. But for the present, as is commonly the case with incipient causes whose effect is incomplete, it complicates all it touches. We still have to consider, after the manner Ricardo began, international trade as one between two or more limits which do not interchange their compound capitals, and then to consider how much the conclusions so drawn are modified by new circumstances and new causes. And as, even when conceived in Ricardo's comparatively simple manner, international trade (as Mr Mill justly said, and as the readers of his discussion on it well know) is an excessively difficult subject of inquiry, we may expect to find many parts of it very hard indeed to reduce to anything like simplicity when new encumbrances are added. The popular discussion of the subject tends to conceal its difficulties, and indeed is mostly conducted by those who do not see them. Nothing is commoner than to see statements on it put forth as axioms which it would take half a book really to prove or disprove. But with the soundness or unsoundness of such arguments I have at present nothing to do. The object of these papers is not to examine the edifice of our English Political Economy, but to define its basis. Nothing but unreality can come of it till we know when and how far its first assertions are true in matter of fact, and when and how far they are not.

THE END.

LONDON: PRINTED BY
SPOTTISWOODE AND CO., NEW-STREET SQUARE
AND PARLIAMENT STREET

）